Brilliant Ideas f
ICT in the Classroom

Brilliant Ideas for Using ICT in the Classroom is a totally practical, hands-on guide to using ICT in and around the classroom for all secondary school teachers and lecturers in post-compulsory education. Assuming no prior expertise, it centres on software and resources that are free or very low cost, and offers step-by-step guidance and creative ideas to improve the experience and engagement of your students.

With a focus on what tools to use, what educational need they satisfy and how to incorporate them into good pedagogy, key topics covered include:

- effective use of presentation technologies
- using, producing and sharing multimedia
- interactive whiteboards and related technologies
- using Web 2.0 technologies
- mobile learning
- supporting diverse student needs through technology.

Brilliant Ideas for Using ICT in the Classroom puts equal emphasis on both technical and pedagogical issues, making it the ideal companion whatever your ICT or e-learning needs. Catering equally well for Windows, Mac and Linux users, this book is designed to give you all the confidence you need to start teaching brilliantly with ICT.

Matt Jarvis is an experienced teacher and trainer, and a Chartered Psychologist. He is author of a range of essential texts for teachers and students and has previously worked as an ILT Co-ordinator. Currently he teaches part-time, runs a small training and consultancy business and has an Honorary Research Fellowship.

Brilliant Ideas for Using ICT in the Classroom

A very practical guide for teachers and lecturers

Matt Jarvis

Routledge
Taylor & Francis Group

LONDON AND NEW YORK

First published 2015
by Routledge
2 Park Square, Milton Park, Abingdon, Oxon OX14 4RN

Simultaneously published in the USA and Canada
by Routledge
711 Third Avenue, New York, NY 10017

Routledge is an imprint of the Taylor & Francis Group, an informa business

British Library Cataloguing in Publication Data
A catalogue record for this book is available from the British
Library

Library of Congress Cataloging in Publication Data
A catalog record for this book has been requested

ISBN: 978-0-415-64049-7 (hbk)
ISBN: 978-0-415-64050-3 (pbk)
ISBN: 978-0-203-08271-3 (ebk)

Typeset in Celeste
by Swales and Willis Ltd, Exeter, Devon, UK

Printed and bound in Great Britain by
TJ International Ltd, Padstow, Cornwall

Contents

Contents

Figures

Figures

Tables

Preface

Welcome to my geeky world! The aim of this book is to provide a totally practical hands-on guide to using ICT to good effect in and around the classroom. In researching this I found lots of academic texts and a few hands-on guides, generally focused on *either* the software *or* how to use it. In putting this book together I wanted to get across something of the three interrelated aspects of educational ICT: what tools to use, what educational need they satisfy and how to incorporate them into good pedagogy. I have therefore divided each section into three parts:

- **The technical bit**: what software to use and a few tips to help you get the best out of it.

- **The theory bit**: just enough educational psychology and/or policy background to give some context to why it might be a good idea to use particular tools in particular ways.

- **The practice**: some suggestions as to how colleagues and I have used ICT in ways that work for us. Note the 'for us'. No-one but you is an expert on what happens in your classroom, and I'm offering ideas rather than prescribing. If it doesn't always read like that, blame my enthusiasm.

I had a couple of other aims in mind when writing this. I worked for a while as a college e-learning co-ordinator with no budget, and I soon worked out that you can do the vast majority of things you'd like to without spending a penny on software. Almost everything I recommend here is free or very low cost, and the majority of tools have an open-source licence – this is a good indicator that they will remain free. In the current climate of austerity low-cost solutions have a whole new significance, but, almost by definition, free stuff doesn't have a marketing budget and awareness of it is shared simply through word of mouth. I aim to save you some time and money by flagging up a good range of free and low-cost tools.

Another personal aim in writing this was to make it relevant to users of a range of operating systems, including both desktop and mobile platforms. Thus users of Mac and Linux as well as Windows should find something useful here. Although almost all UK schools use Windows as their main platform, this is not necessarily true of the individual teacher, who probably does much of their work at home. Moreover, at the time of writing, education is undergoing something of a paradigm shift towards mobile platforms, currently using iPads and Android tablets. The implications of this aren't always well understood, and I will try to clarify what you can and can't (yet) do using mobile platforms alone. Throughout the book I have flagged up what operating systems each of the major tools work on, and tried to recommend tools that work on all the major operating systems. On the odd occasion where this hasn't been possible I have suggested alternatives for each platform.

I hope everyone will find something here that piques their interest or points towards a solution for a problem that was bugging them. Always remember that you, not the hardware or software, are the most important tool, and that your creativity in finding pedagogical solutions, whether or not they involve ICT, is what will make the major difference to your teaching.

I hope you find this useful.

Thanks, Matt

Matt Jarvis, Teacher of Psychology and Health &
Social Care, Totton College; Honorary Research Fellow,
Keele University and Psychology Consultant, National
Science Learning Centre.

CHAPTER 1

Introduction

By the end of this chapter you should be able to:

- disentangle some of the language used to describe educational technology and e-learning;
- consider the use of ICT in the psychological context: fitting technology to how learning happens;
- consider the use of ICT in the policy context: what are we expected to do?;
- acknowledge what ICT can and cannot achieve for your teaching;
- be aware of some factors that might limit your effective use of ICT and some practical strategies to tackle them;
- reflect on the place of ICT in your teaching.

Why do we need a book like this?

Educational technology and e-learning are part of life for the twenty-first-century teacher. Using technology well undoubtedly has the potential to improve learning and teachers' quality of life. In spite of this, however, many teachers still don't speak of technology with affection.

Introduction

Let's get some of the issues and problems out in the open from the outset.

1   There is very little consensus in the teaching profession on what technology we should be using or how best to use it. For one teacher, department or school it might be all about the virtual learning environment, for another the interactive whiteboard is king, and a third will have made the leap to extensive use of a mobile platform. It is hard to have wider professional discussions about the use of technology if we assume we are all doing the same kind of things – we simply aren't.

2   This is easy to say with the benefit of hindsight, but we (by which I mean both managers and e-learning specialists) have largely failed over the last decade to introduce technology well to schools and colleges. By 'well' I mean with a coherent idea of its purpose, with sufficient training in its use and giving teachers a sense of ownership. The result of this has been unnecessary confusion, anxiety and ambivalence, with many teachers seeing technology as much as an additional demand as an opportunity to achieve things.

3   Some teachers are very comfortable with technology and others much less so. Although e-learning evangelists sometimes lose sight of this, it is actually fine! Although you can do wonderfully inspirational and inclusive things with educational technology, the technology is always just a tool and it is neither necessary nor sufficient for brilliant teaching. We enthusiasts should always remember that we have gifted colleagues who achieve just as much using alternative strategies.

Every reader will work in a different context with its own set of priorities and opportunities – and of course demands, frustrations and constraints. There is no one-size-fits-all formula for good practice of e-learning or good use of learning technology, and I haven't tried to prescribe one here. My aim in writing this book has been to introduce a broad range of opportunities so that all readers will take something away from reading this – perhaps a new piece of software, a new teaching technique or just a better understanding of why something you've tried in the past didn't work as you'd hoped. I also hope to remove some of the mystery and anxiety from e-learning. With that in mind, the first section in this chapter is concerned with better understanding the language of technology and e-learning.

The secret language of ICT: is it all Geek to you?

Would you know a Moodle from a Doodle, or Bing from Ning? Technology has proliferated to the extent that it does not have so much its own language as a whole *set* of languages for different specialisms. This esoteric use of language certainly doesn't help those with little technology experience who want to add ICT tools to their teaching toolkit. Here are some of the basics explained.

ICT, ILT, educational technology and e-learning

There is a basic distinction between Information and Communication technology (ICT) and Information and Learning Technology (ILT) or learning technology. *ICT* is a generic term used to describe computing hardware and related communication technology such as telephone systems and networked computers. *ILT* is a fairly broad term that denotes 'the application of IT skills to learning situations using ICT' (National Learning Network, 2004, n.p.). ILT and educational technology can be used interchangeably.

In the last five years terms like ILT and educational technology have fallen out of favour because they imply an emphasis on the technology rather than on teaching and learning. The term *e-learning*, which originally referred to the delivery of whole courses online, is now more commonly used as a generic term to mean the use of technology in an educational context for the purpose of enhancing learning.

CAL and CBL

There is a range of philosophies around as regards to how e-learning should be carried out. In particular there are debates about the extent ICT should fit into the traditional classroom and the extent to which it should shape the learning environments of the future. Broadly, computer-aided learning (CAL) takes place in a fairly traditional classroom. This approach is also sometimes called *technology-enhanced learning*. Computer-*based* learning, by contrast, takes place in a computer suite or students' own homes, with most or all activities being done on computers. Currently (although of course this may change) most developments are in the area of computer-aided learning and this is reflected in the emphasis in this book.

Intranets, CMSs, VLEs and MLEs

An intranet is really just a section of the Internet to which passwords are required for access. It is now the norm for computers in schools and colleges to be networked to form an intranet. Content may be shared on an intranet by means of a content management system (CMS). Content management systems can generally allow approved users to generate web-pages, attach files and communicate by e-mail. A virtual learning environment or VLE is a specialist content management system with education-specific tools for assessment and tracking. VLEs are discussed in more detail on p. 108. A managed learning environment (MLE) includes a VLE and a Management Information System (MIS).

Management Information Systems

All schools and colleges now use database systems to manage information about learners – and increasingly about teachers as well. This is done via a Management Information System or MIS. At one time teachers could safely leave MISs to their management, but increasingly they are now used as the main way to track attendance and achievement. The meaning of MIS had gradually changed so that, where it used to refer to information systems *for managers*, it now refers to systems for the *management of* information by staff at all levels in the institution.

Technology and effective teaching and learning

Using technology may have the potential to improve your teaching. But note the number of conditionals in that sentence! Of course a lot depends on what we mean by improvement. A 2008 JISC report highlights a range of potential benefits to adopting learning technology:

- *Cost and time-saving*: a good quality set of electronic resources can cut down dramatically on preparation time and save on photocopying costs.

Introduction

- *Recruitment and retention*: an attractive and well-organised set of electronic resources can aid recruitment and retention of students.

- *Transferable skills*: familiarising students with a range of ICT applications helps develop their ICT skills for the future.

- *Student achievement*: there is some (limited) evidence to support the idea that judicious use of technology can benefit students in terms of achievement/attainment.

- *Inclusion*: ICT can be used to present material in ways that are compatible with particular styles of information processing, and online resources make education available to students who cannot attend classes because of health problems, social circumstances, disability or geographical factors.

If we think narrowly in terms of education outcomes (i.e. results) then we might be disappointed in the sort of impact we can expect from introducing technology. In a recent review of the impact of technology Machin et al. (2007) concluded that there were wide differences between subjects, with clear evidence to show that technology improves outcomes in some disciplines but not others. Most other reviews have reached rather less flattering conclusions about the impact of technology, and we would be very naive to assume that introducing technological solutions will have much of a direct impact on our results.

Before we get too negative, though, I would suggest that there are at least two sound reasons not to be too disheartened by this failure to demonstrate positive impact. First, it is worth considering the impact of educational technology not only on outcomes but on the learner *experience*. If we can make lessons engaging and congruent with learners' experiences of contemporary culture outside the classroom we are doing something worthwhile, even if this does not lead directly to improvements in our results. There are 'sleeper effects' in teaching and learning, and it is likely that good use of technology in education may have direct impact in the long term, and it is simply difficult to measure this.

Second, and perhaps more important, the fact that introducing new technology does not reliably lead to measurable improvements in outcomes may say far more about the way it has been implemented than it does about its potential to improve learning. If we are simply projecting printed text on a screen instead of writing it on a board, or keeping our handouts on a Virtual Learning Environment instead of a filing cabinet, why on earth would we expect this to make any difference to our learners' progress? Those things may be worth doing because they are convenient, but they don't change the nature of the learning taking place. Using technology to facilitate the kind of activities that really enhance learning is a much more subtle business.

Keeping the focus on principles of effective learning

However sophisticated our understanding of the technical side of educational tech, we should always bear in mind that all technology is simply a set of tools, and that what we do with it should conform to principles of effective learning just like any other mode of teaching. It is easy in our enthusiasm for new software or hardware to forget this (for geeks like me, anyway)!

Developmental psychologist Seymour Papert has pointed out that education has always been a theoretical battleground between two camps. On one hand are those who emphasise the learner's active development of an understanding of the world (we can call these *constructivists*). On the other hand are those who place their emphasis on the curriculum rather than the processes of learning and see teaching and learning more in terms of transmission of information. This approach is sometimes called *instructionism* or the 'transmission' model. As Papert says, the development of learning technology has widened rather than narrowed the gulf between these two philosophical positions. Elsewhere (e.g. Jarvis, 2011) I have tried to abstract from education research a set of broad principles that underlie effective learning and teaching. These are pragmatic and include elements of both instructionist and constructionist positions.

- Learning should be an active process rather than a passive process of taking in information. In the context of e-learning this can be achieved when students use software themselves, for example searching for and presenting information, running simulations or communicating and sharing through social media. Use of popular culture, for example via YouTube, can serve to improve engagement and hence activity levels. Introducing some gentle competition via quizzes can similarly enhance engagement, and there are many technological solutions that lend themselves to facilitating this type of activity.

- Learning should be an interactive process. Interactions take place with teacher, peers and software. Teacher interaction can be in the form of whole-class discussions following the stimulus of a presentation or of scaffolding search, simulation and data analysis tasks. Web 2.0 technologies (see Chapter 5 for a discussion) are designed entirely around the ability to facilitate interaction, and therefore have tremendous and (at the time of writing) largely unexplored potential to enhance learning.

- Learning should be made as relevant as possible to the learner. Something can be relevant because it has personal salience to the learner's life or because it has clear strategic value in supporting the learner's goals. This is a further good reason for involving popular culture in lessons via multimedia technology.

- Learning should be memorable in order to prepare for exams. Material tends to be memorable when it has been deeply processed (i.e. extensively thought about) and visualised, and when recall has been practised. Software can help with all these as long as its use is well planned.

These principles become important when we start to consider some common practices such as using presentation software in the classroom (Chapter 2) or populating a virtual learning environment with handouts (Chapter 5). This is not to say that using presentation software or VLE technology is wrong (far from it!), just that we need to think carefully about these practices in terms of how learning takes place if we want it to impact positively on our learners.

One of the things technophiles have often done wrong is to encourage teachers to work differently in order to accommodate technology. Actually with a bit of lateral thinking we can usually find ways to use technology to help us work in the ways we would like to. Also we should acknowledge that there are some situations where there is no particular advantage to using a high-tech solution, and others where the old-fashioned way is actually the best. If you want to randomly select class members for a task it will always be as quick and effective to draw strips of paper out of an envelope as to use a randomisation app (and requires much less set-up time).

You may face particular issues if you teach subjects where creative thinking and practice are especially valued. English teachers can be forgiven for getting bored with e-learning trainers telling them that texts can be read in electronic format. So what? If that doesn't impact on the quality of the reading experience why should English teachers be impressed? The potential for creativity in multimedia and communication in Web 2.0 applications is much more likely to get creative teachers buzzing.

The policy context

Teachers are great pragmatists and we are no strangers to adapting to what the powers that be (hereafter referred to as PTBs) require us to do. The days when all observed lessons had to involve ICT but no one really minded what you did with it as long as the technology box (Q17 in the 2008 Teaching Standards) could be ticked are gone and not particularly lamented.

The current Teaching Standards (Department for Education, 2012) and current Ofsted Observation Framework (Ofsted, 2012) no longer make direct reference to the use of technology in or around the classroom. At first sight this might seem odd but it is actually quite congruent with a modern understanding of e-learning. It does *not* mean that the importance of technology and e-learning has declined. Rather it means that it is now assumed that our understanding of learning and our use of technology are sufficiently mature that technology can be integrated into teaching and used as and where appropriate. If further evidence is needed that e-learning and educational technology are not out of favour, consider the following quote from Ofsted's 2011 review of ICT in schools:

> In the good and outstanding schools, there were examples of ICT used creatively and imaginatively in many different subject areas by teachers and pupils to bring subjects alive.
>
> (Ofsted, 2011, p. 13)

The emphasis in the current (2012) teaching standards and inspection criteria is on the quality of learning rather than the performance of teaching. We can see this as an opportunity rather than a burden. It frees us up from a box-ticking culture to think creatively about how best to use technology, and better still the emphasis on learner engagement allows us to *have fun.*

What technology can and can't do for your teaching

We need to be realistic about what better use of technology and e-learning can do for our teaching. I have already suggested that use of ICT is neither necessary nor sufficient for good teaching. On the other hand it is well established that well-judged use of tech has the potential to improve the learner experience and to open up education to a more diverse community. For you personally technology may well help you improve personal organisation (for example by organising course materials on a VLE) and help you keep better track of your courses and learner progress (using a Management Information System). If e-learning catches your imagination it can also be an important way of keeping your practice fresh and creative. If you've been teaching for a while it is easy to become jaded, and perhaps the best way to avoid this is to keep finding fresh and creative ways of thinking and working. Technology is an ideal medium for fresh ideas because by its very nature it develops so rapidly.

But let's be brutal for a moment: what will technology probably *not* do for you?

Well, it can't change your personality; it won't make you more empathic or charismatic. If you aren't a 'natural' teacher in terms of personal qualities, you may well be able – with sufficient insight and effort – to develop some, but technology probably won't be the key to doing so. No amount of flashy e-learning techniques will give you the X factor, and no amount of perusing online data about individual learners equates to the sort of listening skills that will really help you understand what makes them tick. If you can't sequence interesting series of activities for your learners then you are unlikely to find inspiration in technological solutions, although you can of course get ideas for individual activities. None of this is meant to be negative, either about human or technological potential. It's simply to say that ICT will always be just one weapon in your armoury, and that there is a lot more to effective teaching than technology.

Practical issues in schools and colleges

Whilst no school, college or Local Authority would deliberately obstruct teachers in the imaginative use of ICT to enhance the quality of learning in or around their lessons, there are in practice a range of local policies and common practices that can conspire to make life more complicated for the e-learning enthusiast than the newbie might expect. Some of the common issues are as follows:

- Different classrooms have different software installed or set as default, so a .docx or video file that works fine in one room won't work, or at least won't work easily, in another. Many teachers have backed away from using technology after the experience of failing to show a video on which a lesson depended, having seen it work earlier in a different room.

- Social websites like YouTube are banned by the institutional or local safeguarding system. This is an understandable response to behaviour management issues, but as long as we think primarily in terms of managing rather than inspiring learners there will be lost opportunities for brilliant activities.

- Subject-relevant websites in general can be similarly difficult to access (I know of at least one LEA that classifies all websites related to my subject – psychology – as occult material and therefore effectively bans access to the subject county-wide).

- Teachers have no rights to install software on their classroom machine or work laptop. In terms of software licensing law this is sensible and protects you as well as the institution from legal problems. It is, however, a real obstacle to innovation.

- There is no easy way to use your own laptop in classrooms, either because connections have been made physically inaccessible or because of unnecessarily restrictive policies.

- Your school has invested heavily in expensive hardware such as class sets of iPads, and now expects all teachers to use them without adequate training or recognition of the individual technological strengths and weaknesses of teachers.

All of these problems are made significantly worse where there is no local technician to help and where everything takes place at the level of the Local Authority. The awkward fact is that all institutions have a duty to balance teacher discretion and the potential gains in learning against concerns over safeguarding and software licensing. There are no panaceas, but you might want to try some of the following strategies to limit the damage caused by local policies that err on the side of caution.

Introduction

- Befriend whoever is responsible for technical support. As an e-learning enthusiast you should be able to find common ground, especially if you show you are aware of the issues from their perspective. Make it clear you understand the issues over software licensing and have the licensing information to hand if you would like anything new installed on a machine.

- As far as possible, ask to have open-source software on school or college machines – this has little or no licensing complications and should go a long way to alleviating the institution's anxiety over software licensing. See Appendix 2 for an explanation of different types of software licence (p. 159). Almost by definition, open-source software is much less likely than commercial alternatives to have a marketing budget, so there may be a learning curve involved here, but licensing as well as its zero cost make open-source a very attractive option.

- Ask for local administrator access to your classroom machine. This will allow you to add and remove software like you would on your own computer. The person responsible will need to be convinced that you understand software licensing issues, but if you are tech-savvy enough to achieve this and to install software yourself it will make your life much easier.

- Whether through local administrator access or a friendly technician, try to make sure a core set of applications are installed in every room you teach in, and that they have any add-ons you need. Old (pre-2007) versions of Microsoft Office require an add-on to handle anything in the .docx or .pptx formats. This is also true of older versions of alternative office software like LibreOffice, so either run a modern version of office software or make sure the add-in is available. VLC or Mplayer, unlike more commonly available multimedia apps, will handle pretty much any video you throw at them, so you shouldn't get any nasty surprises if they are in all your classrooms. Many websites only work properly in particular browsers, so every class-room machine should have at least two browsers that work as differently as possible. Internet Explorer and Firefox are ideal.

- Make sure Flash and Java are kept up-to-date. Your school or college may have an automated network sys-tem for doing this but if it has to be done manually it is worth making sure the person responsible knows you use them regularly. They can then make sure they are up-to-date on machines you use.

- Avoid the temptation to use proxies to gain access to sites like YouTube that may be banned in your institution. This will probably be monitored, and the PTBs may wonder what sites you have been looking at! Depending on how web content is filtered in your institution it may be possible to unblock sites just on your machine. Otherwise you may be limited to what you have downloaded in advance of a lesson. That's okay as long as your planning is sufficiently organised.

Conclusions and reflections

Reflect for a moment on where you stand with regard to education technology. Are you an enthusiast or more wary? Are you frankly terrified? At one extreme, Seymour Papert (1996) has identified the 'cyberostrich', who buries their head in the sand and ignores the potential afforded by educational technology. At the other extreme is the

Introduction

'cyberlemming' (Jarvis, 2011), who hurls themself into using technology without due consideration of its implications for effective learning and teaching. As a cyberostrich you can be a perfectly competent (or even brilliant) teacher, but you will probably be missing a few tricks. As a cyberlemming you risk derailing your teaching altogether, but as long as you learn quickly enough from your mistakes you may become an expert. We all fall somewhere on the spectrum between ostrich and lemming, and being aware of this can help you plan the sort of e-learning that will work for you.

Consider as well what you would like to use ICT for. Or to turn that around, what aspects of your practice do you want to work on? If you want to develop more interesting tasks for your learners outside the classroom then you might want to focus on VLE or Web 2.0 technology. If you are concerned that your students are missing out on opportunities to visualise complex images like a molecule or the human body you might do well to consider advanced presentation techniques. If you want to develop more classroom interactivity think in terms of quiz software and perhaps specialist subject software. You may have something else altogether in mind. The point is, you don't have to master all the technology available; just find the thing that can help you achieve what you want to.

CHAPTER 2

Presenting on a screen

By the end of this chapter you should be able to:

- know of PowerPoint and other linear presentation tools, including free and online alternatives;
- understand some common problems with linear presentation tools and be aware of strategies for working effectively with them;
- consider non-linear presentation tools such as Prezi, and appreciate when they may be the tools of choice for classroom presentations;
- use more interactive tools like VUE and Whyteboard;
- understand how and when to project PDFs;
- consider ways to combine presentation technologies;
- consider the usefulness of interactive whiteboard technology.

Once upon a time teaching largely consisted of writing on a board at the front of the classroom. This practice was based on a 'transmission model' of teaching and learning, in which teachers pass on information to learners. Although pedagogy has moved on from the transmission model and teaching is a much less didactic business than it used to be, we still find ourselves regularly projecting information on to a screen. The data projector has partially replaced the board pen, and in this history lies a problem. We can project all sorts of information on to a screen, but as a legacy of the chalk-and-talk era what we actually tend to do is project dense verbal information. This may be a mistake, and this chapter is as much about *what* to project as how to. Let's first take a look at PowerPoint presentations.

Better PowerPoint presentations

The technical bit

The industry standard software for presentations is PowerPoint, part of the Microsoft Office Suite. It is the most commonly used presentation tool in education, industry and just about everywhere. It is also the most commonly used piece of software in the classroom.

Table 2.1 Key app: PowerPoint

Publisher	Microsoft	www.microsoft. com	Licence: Commercial
Platform	Windows YES	Mac YES	Linux YES (with WINE)
Also consider	LibreOffice Impress (Windows, Mac, Linux), Thinkfree.com (online)		
Mobile situation	Microsoft 365 online available for iOS and android. Free alternatives include Kingsoft Office suite		

In the 1990s the first wave of e-learning arrived in the classroom, and there was great enthusiasm for using PowerPoint as an alternative to the traditional board for delivering information. Although there were undoubtedly honourable exceptions, many of us fell into a classic cyberlemming trap! Teachers soon found that giving presentations in this way discouraged student activity and interactivity, and as a result the quality of learning declined rather than improved.

The theory bit

Following its early adoption as a classroom tool there has since been something of a backlash against PowerPoint, criticisms being summed up in the bluntly titled article 'PowerPoint is evil' (Tufte, 2004). PowerPoint:

- encourages simplistic thinking by summarising complex ideas on to a slide in the form of bullet points or graphs;
- is often used as a cue to remind a teacher of their next point rather than as an aid for the audience;
- encourages teachers to restructure content so that each idea fits on a slide;
- encourages classes to read material only in the order in which it is presented. This can be a disadvantage for students with particular information-processing styles.

PowerPoint looks like a tool for making business presentations – because that's primarily what it is. Before being bought up and developed by Microsoft PowerPoint was developed by engineers for the purpose of condensing complex technical information for a business audience. Psychologist Ian Kinchington (2006) uses JJ Gibson's theory of direct perception to understand why we tend to use it in the same way in education. In the same way that we recognise a chair as a chair because its appearance contains enough information to tell us that it *affords* sitting, we recognise PowerPoint as a business presentation tool because it *affords* listing dense bullet points. Unless we make a conscious effort to take control, we tend to respond to the

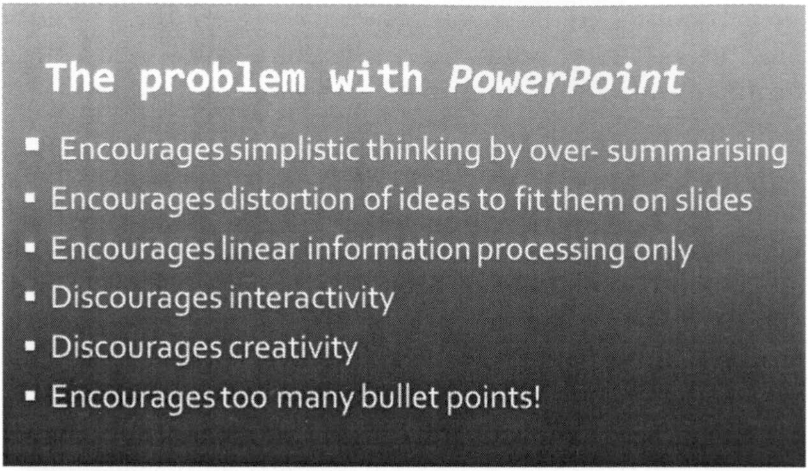

Figure 2.1 A typical PowerPoint slide

PowerPoint interface by giving a business pitch rather than a lesson. Figure 2.1 shows a fairly typical PowerPoint slide. There is too much information here, it is all verbal and it is all organised in the form of bullet points.

This sort of presentation is also rather a waste of technology! If we are projecting dense verbal information on to a board, in spite of obvious superficial differences, the learner is essentially processing information in exactly the same way as if the teacher wrote on a board with chalk.

Information on a PowerPoint slide will generally be in either verbal or visual form. Paivio's dual coding theory predicts that information will be better retained when presented in both visual and verbal forms, while theories of learning styles predict that some students will benefit more from visual information and others more from verbal information. Either way students probably benefit from having a good balance of visual and verbal information. We tend to use too much verbal and not enough visual information.

Figure 2.2 If we are just projecting dense verbal information we might as well use a chalk board!

Although the unvaried use of bulleted text is the classic error, adding more visual information won't help if there is too much of it. Consider the slide of the military situation in Afghanistan in Figure 2.3.

Confused? Almost certainly. US General McChrystal reportedly said on seeing this slide that 'when we understand that slide we'll have won the war'.

PowerPoint can also be boring. The human mind simply doesn't find reading dense bulleted text interesting. As Educational Psychologist Sean Cameron points out, if Churchill had had PowerPoint Britain would probably have lost World War II! It is hard to inspire with PowerPoint unless we diverge considerably from the business presentation model.

One common practice that both adds to boredom and may even make information harder to learn is to read aloud from slides. This prevents us speaking directly to

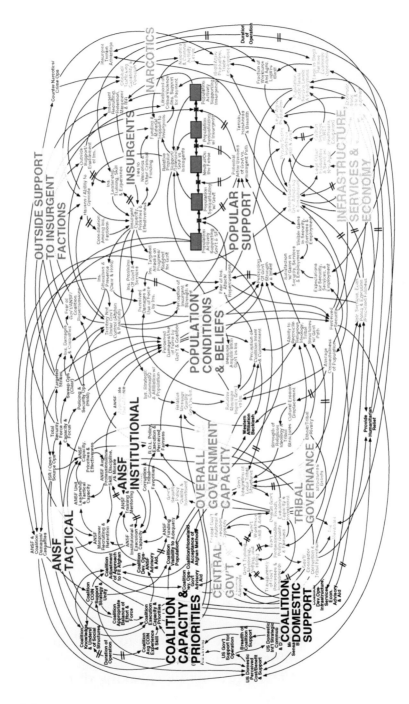

Figure 2.3 A US military representation of the situation in Afghanistan

and interacting with our students and, if the information is dense, it may also increase cognitive load because listeners have to simultaneously use the auditory and visual channels in their short-term memory to process the same information (Maag, 2004). This sort of inefficient information processing can interfere with learning.

The practice

PowerPoint is just a tool, and actually from a technical point of view it's a pretty good one. We just need to think a bit laterally about how to put it to best use in the classroom. From this perspective the current backlash against PowerPoint per se is not really justified. As Peter Norvig (2003) puts it, 'PowerPoint doesn't kill teaching and learning. Teachers and lecturers kill teaching and learning. But using PowerPoint is like having a loaded AK-47 machine gun on the desk: you can do very unpleasant things with it' (2003, p. 343). There are, however, a number of ways to avoid doing unpleasant things.

Use presentations as a stimulus rather than to deliver the bulk content

We tend to think of PowerPoint as a tool for content delivery. Actually it is equally suited to projecting an interesting image or quote that can serve as a 'fascinator' starter activity. One simple strategy is to use PowerPoint for really short presentations, for example for showing stimulus material at the start of a lesson or topic. This need not even contain words, let alone bullet points. Imagery, music and film can interest, inspire and trigger emotional responses from students at least as well as words. Of course it may be that once you decide to project something other than heavy content, you decide that PowerPoint is not necessarily the right tool.

23

Presenting on screen

Figure 2.4 Short, stimulating presentations may be a better bet than long, content-heavy ones

Note as well that under the Ofsted (2012) inspection framework it is now much harder to justify long content-heavy presentations in an observed lesson.

Vary the format

If you are going to use PowerPoint for longer and more technical expositions, try the following strategies to vary the form in which information is perceived:

- Use images, not just in the corner of a slide to add variety, but as whole slides to make a point or stimulate discussion.

- Embed or link to video. You may decide of course to run a media tool alongside your presentation tool rather than put the whole content in the presentation.

Make slides interactive

- Put questions, quotes, exercises and discussion points on slides as well as information, and make sure you stop talking to give students time to think; PowerPoint affords lecturing but you can resist the temptation! There is no reason why lessons based around a presentation can't be a much more interactive process.

You can also make a presentation-based lesson more interactive by taking questions and comments. This need not require the use of technology, but there are advantages in some cases to a techy solution, in particular where you have shy learners that might not interact in a whole-class context. You can take feedback and questions electronically using an online blogging or collaborative editing tool. I like Collabedit (http://collabedit.com) because you don't have to register and because you can post questions from a Smartphone. However, depending on the context in which you are working you may prefer to deliberately avoid this! In that case something like PrimaryPad might suit you better.

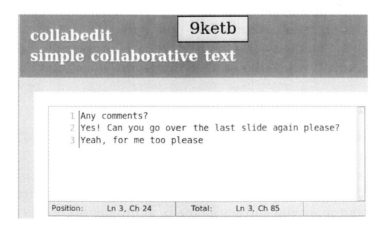

Figure 2.5 If you run collabedit or something similar alongside a presentation you can take real-time questions and comments

Presenting on screen

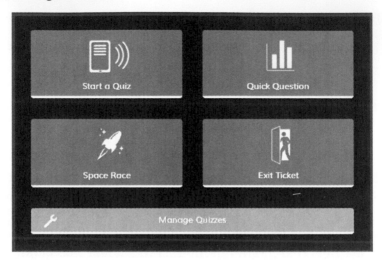

Figure 2.6 Socrative

You can also make presentations interactive by using an app called Socrative (www.socrative.com). This is an online substitute for the clumsy and expensive learner response systems that have allowed polling and quizzing of learners for a while now. Socrative has a teacher app with which you set up questions to poll, quiz and assess learner progress. Students have a different app on their phones or tablets with which they can log in to your questions.

Think really carefully before using bullet points

Bullet points are the obvious way to structure a slide and are not always inappropriate, but they are overused. Try a radial model of boxes and arrows, as in figure 2.7, to create a more visually interesting slide. You may want to use concept-mapping software (see p. 35) to generate this sort of display and either use that instead of PowerPoint or export an image of the concept map to put on a slide.

Use animation wisely

Too much animation just adds to cognitive load and makes it harder for learners to retain the content of a slide, but it is really helpful to be able to call up one packet of information on-screen, explain it, then call up the next, rather than presenting a whole slide's worth of information in one hit.

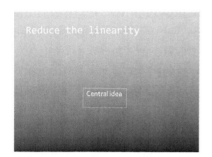 

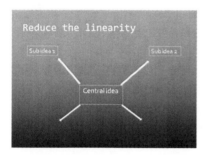 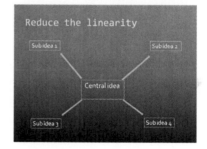

Figure 2.7 An animated slide with a non-traditional format

This can be one, of course, with a bulleted slide, however it lends itself well to radial designs like the one shown in Figure 2.7.

Alternative linear presentation tools

Although PowerPoint is the best-known and most widely used linear presentation tool, there are a variety of alternatives that do essentially the same thing. In particular it is worth considering free and online tools.

Impress (part of the LibreOffice and OpenOffice suites)

This is an open-source alternative to PowerPoint. Although (at least at the time of writing) the Impress interface is more traditional than that of the 2007+ PowerPoint, its functionality is very similar. The main advantage of Impress is that it is free. This can be important in widening participation; depending on where you teach you may well find that you are limited in your ability to set students homework involving creating presentations by the fact that some students do not have access to PowerPoint at home.

ThinkFree (www.thinkfree.com/)

There are a number of online presentation tools around. Being online means these can be accessed from any computer. Of the free ones ThinkFree is perhaps the most powerful and versatile of these (at least at the time of writing), providing many of the same functions as PowerPoint and Impress. ThinkFree allows you to upload existing PowerPoint files to edit and to download your presentations in PowerPoint format. Like Impress, ThinkFree is free and so can serve a purpose in widening participation. The interface is very familiar so there is a shallow learning curve for those used to PowerPoint.

Using Prezi: a non-linear presentation tool

The technical bit

Prezi is a very different presentation tool. It can be run free online or there is a commercial desktop version.

For a long time teachers and others who give presentations have looked for a genuine alternative to linear tools like PowerPoint. A limitation of traditional tools like PowerPoint is their linearity. We have to choose in advance the order in which we present ideas, and it is relatively awkward to diverge from this order in response to the needs of your audience. Prezi has a very different philosophy. Instead of separate slides a Prezi presentation has a single zoomable canvas.

A path can be inserted between text, images, video, etc., so you can use Prezi in a linear fashion like PowerPoint,

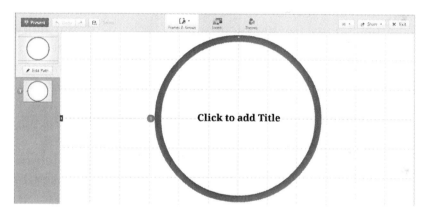

Figure 2.8 The Prezi interface

Table 2.2 Key app: Prezi

Publisher	Prezi.inc	www.prezi.com	Licence: Commercial	
Platform	Windows YES	Mac YES	Linux YES	Online YES
Also consider	Sozi (this is in an early stage of development at the time of writing)			
Mobile situation	Currently available for iOS but not Android			

however you can zoom in and out at will, diverging from your path or not having one in the first place. This makes Prezi much more flexible when you want learners to lead the direction of a discussion and you don't know what order you will want to present ideas in.

The theory bit

Recall Ian Kinchington's points about affordances and the linearity of PowerPoint (p. 19). A PowerPoint presentation determines the order in which points are put across and this tends to be one point at a time. The zooming canvas approach is a way to escape this kind of information processing. Seeing the big picture then focusing down more narrowly on an idea within it is probably a much better representation of the way we naturally process information than the linear approach afforded by PowerPoint. Because Prezi makes use of logical, visual and spatial information it may also help cater for learners with a range of information processing styles (Manning et al., 2011).

In addition learners can regularly see the 'big picture' throughout a presentation. This in turn can be used to ensure that learners keep the objectives of a lesson in mind – much more effective than showing objectives at the beginning and end of a presentation. If PowerPoint affords simplifying a complex area, then Prezi affords *exploring* it.

If Prezi helps learners take control of the direction of a discussion then it also facilitates active learning, not just in the sense of learners doing things in lessons but also in the sense of active decision-making. When a group of learners is presented with the whole of a zoomed-out topic they can explore it by selecting areas to focus down on and choosing the order in which to tackle ideas. This kind of active decision-making is required in the current Ofsted framework and much harder to achieve using linear tools like PowerPoint. Where material is actively explored it is likely to be more 'deeply' processed and therefore better remembered.

The practice

Prezi can incorporate the same variety of media as PowerPoint. Thus text, images, sound and video can be dropped into a presentation, with the same potential for multisensory processing. The overriding question among teachers accustomed to PowerPoint as the tool of choice is 'when is there a real advantage to using Prezi?'

When ideas are being explored

Prezi is useful whenever an idea is to be explored. For example, in English, word charts allow learners to take a word and explore its synonyms, antonyms, etc. Geographers can zoom in to areas on a map in Prezi. This would not be possible in PowerPoint.

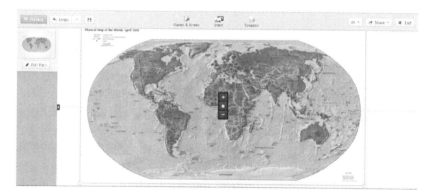

Figure 2.9 With a Prezi map, learners can make choices about where to zoom in to and you can choose the tasks or information they find when they select

Presenting on screen

When we want students to think creatively

Linear processing of information can work reasonably well when we want to take students through logical progressions of ideas – like the stages of an equation. However, this sort of information processing is the antithesis of creativity, the lifeblood of some subjects, for example English. This may be one reason why (as any e-learning trainer will tell you!) English teachers are often the most resistant to incorporating technology into their teaching. Those who place particular value on creativity may sense intuitively when technology does not support it.

Prezi, on the other hand, with its ability help learners see the big picture and explore areas within it, facilitates much more flexible and creative ways of thinking. A Prezi presentation may thus be a good stimulus when we are cuing learners in to carry out a creative task. Prezi also lends itself to assessment, as it allows learners to take a topic and explore the relationships between its elements. If you set learners the task of producing presentations, try getting them to use Prezi rather than PowerPoint. You may find them more inspired and creative than you expect.

When we want to support a free-flowing discussion

There are times when as teachers we want to constrain discussion of a complex or controversial topic, leading students down particular lines of enquiry. However, when there is no good reason to constrain discussion we may be better off using a non-linear presentation tool like Prezi that allows us to zoom in on material that supports points as they emerge. Say you were discussing politics. You have no idea in what order learners will raise different viewpoints, and the flow of such a discussion might be ruined by the constraints of PowerPoint. However, with a Prezi in the

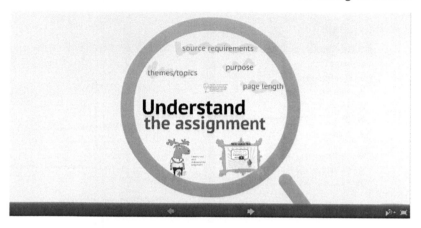

Figure 2.10 Prezis can support free-flowing discussion with
supporting information

background you can zoom into supporting information as required.

Combining PowerPoint and Prezi

A further strength of Prezi is that you can show a PowerPoint presentation as part of your Prezi presentation. At the time of writing there are three ways to do this, allowing varying degrees of sophistication. The simplest way is to directly import the .ppt or .pptx file into Prezi. This will place your slides or a selection of them in your Prezi presentation. Slides will effectively be separate images. However, if you export your PowerPoint as a Shockwave Flash (.swf) file you can import this into your Prezi and it will run, showing successive slides at each click. This approach still won't show animations however. A third approach is to screen-record your PowerPoint running in presentation mode and to insert this as a video into your Prezi. This is the most technical and fiddly option but the only way (at the time of writing) to preserve your animation.

Presenting on screen

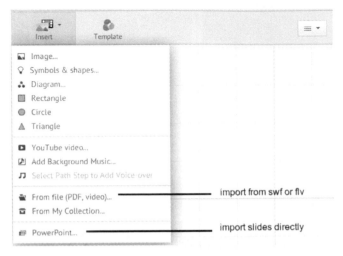

Figure 2.11 Options for inserting PowerPoint slides into a Prezi

Using a concept map presenter

The technical bit

There are a number of concept mapping tools around, both free and commercial. They have a number of applications in education, but in this chapter we are concerned with their usefulness as a presentation tool. VUE is particularly useful for presenting because it is zoomable and has a presentation mode. The VUE interface is shown in Figure 2.12.

Table 2.3 Key app: VUE

Publisher	Tufts University	http://vue.tufts.edu	Licence: Free & open-source
Platform	Windows YES	Mac YES	Linux YES
Also consider	Xmind (full version with presentation mode is commercial)		
Mobile situation	Not available for iOS or Android		

Figure 2.12 The VUE interface

To use VUE you insert nodes, which may contain text, images or links to online content, then create connections between your nodes. At the time of writing VUE is less visually slick than PowerPoint or Prezi, however it really lends itself to learner participation and to creating a well-structured visual resource.

The theory bit

Novak (1964) developed the idea of concept-mapping. His starting point was the idea that new knowledge is based on existing knowledge. If we start with a concept that we already know about then learning takes place as we explore that concept and add to our knowledge. As teachers we can provide an 'expert skeleton', that is, a basic concept map that learners can build upon. This ensures that although students are actively exploring an idea, they do so along prescribed lines that tie in with the ways in which that knowledge is going to be assessed. An example of an expert skeleton is shown in Figure 2.13. Novak and Canas (2006) recommend that learners are given an expert skeleton as a starting point and that they then work collaboratively to develop it. This ensures that learning is both active and interactive.

Presenting on screen

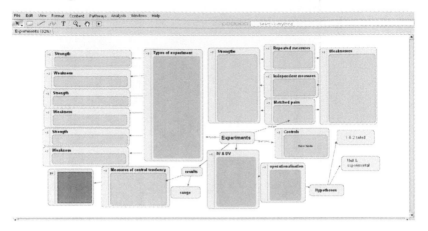

Figure 2.13 An expert skeleton for exploring the experimental method

The practice

Concept maps can be used in a number of ways, but here we are concerned with VUE as a presentation tool. VUE is wasted if we use it to simply present a path from node to node, as we can produce a nicer looking connected node structure in Prezi or even PowerPoint. VUE comes into its own when we want learners to construct their own representation of a concept, or to apply their own higher level thinking skills to a topic. The presentation function of VUE is important because it allows learners to take ownership of particular nodes and present them to larger groups. It is therefore a great tool for reciprocal teaching or jigsawing lessons.

Take the concept map in Figure 2.13. A science class can divide into smaller groups, each of which takes responsibility for an aspect of the experimental method. When this is thoroughly explored each small group can present their node to the rest of the group using VUE's zoom function (see Figure 2.14b). When each group has completed this process the large group will have a complete visual representation of the topic.

Figure 2.14a In a 'jigsaw' lesson on the experimental method a small group completes their node using a laser keyboard

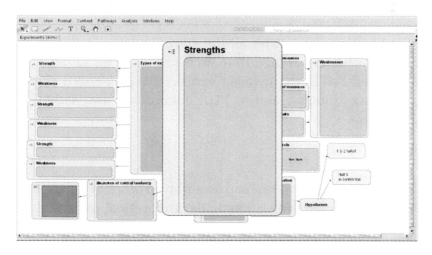

Figure 2.14b They present their node to the whole class

Using a flipchart simulator

The technical bit

Whyteboard is a free piece of software that is variously described as a painting tool, a PDF annotator and interactive whiteboard software. I prefer to think of it as a flipchart simulator. Flipcharts are still used extensively in some settings because they provide a lot more flexibility than most technological apps in allowing a teacher or facilitator to record what learners say in response to questions.

Table 2.4 Key app: Whyteboard

Publisher	Sourceforge	https://launchpad.net/whyteboard	Licence: Free & open-source
Platform	Windows YES	Mac YES	Linux YES
Also consider	Commercial interactive whiteboard packages		
Mobile situation	Not available for iOS or Android		

Whyteboard provides all the spontaneity of a flipchart, but with the advantage that each page can be saved as a PDF. You can draw or place text on a Whyteboard sheet, and insert images, audio, PDF documents and video, if applicable.

The theory and practice

Unlike the other non-linear presentation tools, Whyteboard is not associated with a particular theoretical perspective. As a flipchart simulator it is more of a pragmatic attempt to maintain a traditional and successful way of working using modern technology.

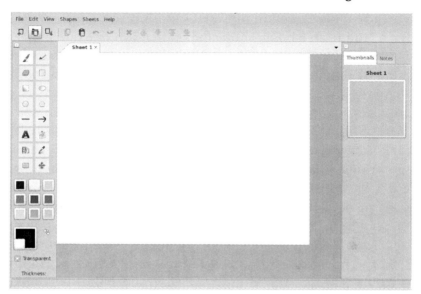

Figure 2.15 The Whyteboard interface

Whyteboard is useful for any discussion situation where you want the freedom to record points as they arise. It becomes the tool of choice where you have no preconceived ideas of a structure for the ideas. Where there is such a structure then Prezi or VUE will probably work better. Whyteboard also comes into its own where you or a student have mobility problems and cannot easily write on a board. With a laptop or mobile keyboard on your desk you can sit still and face a class as you write. Depending on the context you work in this may help with class management. With a mobile keyboard a student can contribute to what is on screen without moving.

Presenting PDFs

PDFs are documents and not really designed to be presented on a screen. However, there are times when you may wish to show a section of a PDF on a presentation screen, for example an e-book, subject specification or exam paper. If you are looking to show a short document like an exam paper the major functionality you need is to be able to zoom in and out. This allows you to take a small section such as a single exam question in font size 12 and fill the screen with it. Having a full screen mode and the ability to highlight text are welcome bonus features. Standard PDF readers like Adobe Reader and Foxit Reader will allow simple presentations with these features perfectly well. There is also software out there marketed specifically as being for PDF presentation, but at the time of writing this tends not to have zoom functionality and so is actually fairly redundant.

Sometimes, for example when talking learners through a specification or showing several extracts from an e-book, you might want the additional functionality to be able to select rapidly from and move between a large number of pages. For this I recommend Prezi. If you load a PDF into a Prezi presentation it will display each page as a separate zoomable node. Prezi is infinitely flexible in its zooming; you can create a frame to zoom in to and this can be as small as a single word or as large as a chapter. You can also highlight documents. An example is shown in Figure 2.16.

Combining the use of presentation tools

On occasion you may find yourself running a complex lesson involving a Prezi, a couple of PowerPoint presentations and a video. If you are using an operating system with the ability to run multiple desktops, for example Mac or Linux, seamlessly switching between apps is straightforward and visually slick. However, in a UK school the chances are that you are using Windows, in which switching between apps is a more clunky business. There are a couple of solutions to this if you would like to slicken the process. First and most

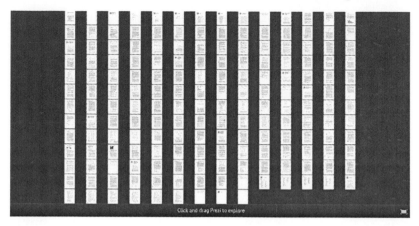

Figure 2.16 A zoomable PDF e-book in Prezi

obviously, you can embed PowerPoint presentations and video into a Prezi (this is explained on p. 35).

Alternatively you can now also combine PowerPoint presentations, Prezis, PDFs and video into a single presentation using a (Windows-only at the time of writing) app called SlideDog (www.slidedog.com). This is described on the website as 'free for casual use'. There are also commercial apps that allow you to incorporate a Prezi into a PowerPoint, but at the time of writing I haven't seen anything free or low-cost.

Interactive whiteboards: to IWB or not to IWB?

Teachers are quite divided about the use of interactive whiteboards, and we might have to conclude that this is an issue over which good people can and do disagree. A major factor affecting our personal views is how we were first introduced to the technology. When introducing a major new piece of technology into the Private Sector it is standard practice to spend five to ten times as much on training as on the technology itself. This is usually not the case in education, and many of us involved in e-learning management badly underestimated the kind of training and practice required before teachers can use IWB tech to its potential.

A lot also depends on your subject and level. Where existing packages can be bought off the shelf, using an IWB can be the 'easy' way to deliver a lesson. However, these packages are expensive to develop so most work goes into producing packages for courses with very large numbers. In minority subjects where teachers have to develop resources from scratch, IWBs are sometimes viewed with less affection as they increase rather than reduce preparation time. What this means in practice is that while some teachers enhance the quality of their learners' experiences tremendously using IWBs, in many other classrooms the IWB is either treated as a projector screen or ignored entirely.

The technical bit

IWBs are interactive displays that connect to a computer and projector (some newer devices have an integrated projector). The board itself serves simultaneously as a screen and input device. You project on to the board but it is also touch-responsive and you can operate the software by touching the board. Standard software for web browsing, presentations and multimedia can be operated on an IWB by touch; however, there is also IWB software that allows a range of extra functionality. Some of this is generic and some subject-specific. Some things you can do with IWB software in addition to what could be done using more standard tools on a non-interactive screen (or at least do more easily) include:

- move objects around a screen (drag and drop)
- hide and reveal objects

- highlight objects

- animate objects

- store and retrieve information

- generate feedback when objects are selected.

(adapted from Glover et al., 2005)

Because IWBs come as a hardware-software package they are all commercially produced. The market is dominated by two systems, Smart and Promethean. There are significant differences in both their hardware and software. If you get a say in which system ends up in your classroom it would be well worth investing some time in exploring which you think you will prefer. If you are making a purchasing decision at the institutional level, do your research. This is *not* to say one system is superior, just that they feel more different than you might expect and

Figure 2.17 Smart Boards have distinctive coloured electronic 'pens'

43

that you personally will probably have a distinct preference once you have explored them a bit.

The theory bit

IWBs were not developed with a particular theoretical underpinning; however, there is no shortage of literature seeking to understand them in terms of education theory or to evaluate their impact. In a literature review Miller et al. (2005) reports that IWBs can support visual and kinaesthetic learning styles, improve learner attention and motivation, support multimedia and facilitate questioning. However, some of these positive conclusions have been challenged. The idea of kinaesthetic and visual learners has fallen out of favour since the Miller review, and later studies have suggested that although IWBs do facilitate questioning they are not associated with improvements in learner *engagement* with questions.

There is also evidence to suggest that in many cases introduction of IWBs is associated with an increase in the time spent in whole-class teaching at the expense of more student-centred teaching styles (Higgins et al., 2005). This can be understood in terms of Kinchington's idea of technological affordances. Like PowerPoint, IWBs look like tools designed to focus attention on the teacher and the front of the classroom, therefore that is how we tend to use them. This is not an argument against IWB technology, just a reminder of the importance of thinking beyond the obvious and keeping principles of effective learning at the heart of how we use technology.

The practice

IWBs can be used in so many ways in different subjects and levels that it is very difficult to prescribe a 'one size fits all' way of working. What is possible, though, is to look at IWBs in the context of current education policy and the principles of effective learning, and make a few very general recommendations.

Keep it active and interactive

As when using PowerPoint, it is tempting to slip into a lecturing style when using an IWB. Remember that, although you can do whizzy things on an IWB that are superficially more attractive and engaging than most of what you can do without one, if your learners are taking a passive role this engagement may not lead to particularly improved learning. You can avoid this temptation, however; just remember that if a demonstration does not directly lead to high levels of activity or interactivity that you:

- keep it brief and make sure learners know why you are doing it and what they need to get from the demonstration;
- follow it up immediately with something more active/interactive.

Bear in mind as well that the current orthodoxy is that whole-class interactive teaching is not sufficiently active or interactive on its own, and that at some point any whole-class discussion of something you have just demonstrated on an IWB should be followed up by pair or group work. This is probably a fashion that will move on in time; however, watching this can make a big difference to an observed lesson grade! Also remember that although IWBs lend themselves to quizzes, especially when used in conjunction with a learner response system, the current guidelines for questioning favour elaborated answers rather than the fast, snappy answers that this sort of tech normally encourages.

Don't reinvent the wheel unless you want to

Check out what existing IWB resources exist for your subject and age group. Some of these are in standard formats and, although they are designed with IWBs in mind, may be of use to you using a traditional projector and screen. These may be available from a range of commercial suppliers, but do also consider community resource-sharing sites. www.iwb.org.uk is a popular generic repository, but others exist specialising in particular levels and subjects. Your subject will have a professional association, and some of these provide a facility for swapping IWB resources.

Think about what software you are using on the IWB

Sometimes a little lateral thinking goes a long way. We are not limited to using bespoke IWB software, nor do we need to revert to seeing an IWB as a glorified screen for projecting PowerPoint presentations on to. Consider the other tools discussed in this chapter. The combination of zooming and touch capability makes Prezi a good choice for learner-selected quiz questions, for example. Using VUE, learners might move nodes around a concept map or draw in links.

What if you don't have an IWB?

However convenient and impressive IWB technology can be, it is neither necessary nor sufficient for good teaching and learning. In fact, some tasks often performed using an IWB can be done at least as easily without one if you have a reasonable knowledge of alternative strategies – which may be high or low tech. If what we want from an IWB is the ability for learners to come to the front of the room and interact with the board, consider whether you can carry out the same activity with a tablet or even a mobile keyboard and/or mouse. If these mean the learner doesn't have to leave their seat this has advantages for those with limited mobility and for learners who feel exposed at the front of the room.

Learner response systems, which link to an IWB and allow learners to contribute answers to quizzes or collaborative activities, are engaging. They also keep score automatically, which can be an advantage, depending on the activity. However, consider the cost of these systems added to that of the IWB. I would want to know how much use and how much concrete advantage I would be getting from these before shelling out several thousand pounds. It is also worth considering what other technology you could spend the money on for a classroom. It is likely that many – though in fairness not all – teachers would get at least as much from having two projectors with separate computers running simultaneously or perhaps a set of netbooks or tablets for learners at less cost.

Conclusions and reflections

When we think 'presentation' we tend to think about PowerPoint, and we tend to think about using PowerPoint in quite narrow ways. I advocate using both PowerPoint (or an equivalent like Impress) in non-traditional ways and alternate tools for different situations. Prezi is visually interesting and facilitates creative thinking and free-flowing discussion. Where you have an expert skeleton in mind and are looking for learner participation in exploring/completing this, VUE is ideal, and where you simply want to note points as they arise without any pre-existing structure, then Whyteboard becomes the tool of choice.

Presenting on screen

Perhaps most importantly, whatever tool you are using, remember that it is only ever a medium, and that there are few if any situations in modern education where there is a place for a traditional business-style presentation. Presentation tools work best when they are used to stimulate active and interactive learning. They are neither necessary nor sufficient to achieve this, but, used well, they can enhance the learner experience.

This is perhaps even truer of interactive whiteboard technology, although IWBs are used so differently – and to different effect – in different subjects at different levels in different institutions that it is very hard to make generalisations. IWBs can be very powerful tools in the right context, but they are an expensive bit of kit, and an awful lot of money has been spent exploring their potential, as often as not without success.

CHAPTER 3

Working more imaginatively with text

By the end of this chapter you should be able to:

- appreciate the importance of thinking about the quality of written resources for learners;
- be aware of a range of text-handling tools including word processing, desktop publishing and document processing software;
- understand the benefits of using PDFs and be familiar with tools for reading, creating and editing them;
- be able to incorporate a range of features into text documents including graphics, interactive exercises and a range of linguistic features into text resources;
- locate sources of free images and be familiar with some tools for simple image editing.

With so much exciting multimedia about it is easy to neglect the humble handout. However, there is a lot you can do to improve the experience of your learners when they work with text documents. This is a lot more than an indulgence for learners; in the modern world we are all likely to encounter text in a magazine, textbook or online, and publishers of all these media have cottoned on to the fact that it is much easier to read and make sense of attractively laid out, bite-sized chunks of text interspersed with other media. In that social context we are fighting a losing battle if we expect our learners to wade through dense, badly laid out handouts. We can address this, however; we just need an understanding of some text- and image-handling tools and some theoretical understanding of what a good text resource should look like.

Producing text

The technical bit

There are more ways than you might think to put text on a page. We will all have worked with word processing packages, but you might also want to consider desktop publishing and document processing software for particular tasks. I also think there are advantages to working with PDFs – but only if you can do what you want with them! It is therefore worth exploring software for working with PDFs.

Word processing

The first thing you will need for any kind of textual work is a word processing application. The industry standard software is Microsoft's Word, part of the Office suite. This is so omnipresent and well understood that I won't waste space going over the basics here. I would draw your attention, however, to a free and open-source alternative, Writer. This is part of the LibreOffice and OpenOffice packages. This has most of the functionality of Word, and many people find its traditional layout much easier to use than that of recent versions of Word. In terms of widening participation Writer has the huge advantage of being free and is worth recommending to students who might have no access to MS Office or access to a very dated version.

Figure 3.1 The Microsoft Word interface

Figure 3.2 The LibreOffice Writer interface

One complication you'll soon come across working with modern word processors is document formats. This is not well known but there is an internationally agreed Open Document Text format (ODT). However, most people use the proprietary Microsoft formats .doc or .docx. Free apps like Writer tend to handle .doc perfectly and .docx reasonably well. Older versions of MS Word tend to have difficulty with open document files. The .docx format – the standard Word format since 2007 – has made new functionality like SmartArt available; however, it has caused compatibility problems with many other apps including those that work online. A tip is to only save with a .docx suffix if you are sure the document is going to be opened by someone with up-to-date MS Office and not uploaded to a website.

Desktop publishing

Word processors will handle basic handouts and worksheets just fine; however, there are times when you want something a bit more impressive – such as when you (or better still your learners) want to produce a poster or flyer. This is where desktop publishing comes into its own. Scribus is a free and open-source application that, because of the nature of its design, is friendly enough for beginners but fully featured enough to appeal to some professionals.

Table 3.1 Key app: Scribus

Publisher	Scribus	www.scribus.net	Licence: Free and open-source
Platform	Windows YES	Mac YES	Linux YES
Also consider	Microsoft Publisher (commercial)		
Mobile position	Not available for iOS or Android		

Figure 3.3 The Scribus interface

In Scribus you can work with text, images, etc., as you do with a word processor, but you have rather more control over the final product, so you can produce more attractive documents. Save your completed document as a PDF for easy opening and printing on other machines.

Document processing

Have you ever looked at a journal publication and wondered how it looks so professional in spite of having relatively few text features? Just by having really well thought-out line spacing, heading formats, etc., they manage to make a simple piece of text appear visually interesting. Many people in publishing use a format called LaTeX to achieve this level of slickness. To produce LaTeX to a really high standard requires learning a programming language; however, there is a shortcut to producing this sort of professional-looking text resource. This is called document processing software – I recommend Lyx, which is free and open-source, and available for all major operating systems.

Table 3.2 Key app: Lyx

Publisher	Lyx.org	www.lyx.org	Licence: Free & open-source
Platform	Windows YES	Mac YES	Linux YES
Also consider	I wouldn't – Lyx is currently well ahead of the game		
Mobile position	Not available for iOS or Android		

A document processor like Lyx takes plain text and formats it according to a set of predetermined rules. Essentially it frees you up from making decisions about format and allows you to simply write content. Unless you are a design professional the output from a document processor like Lyx will probably be slicker than anything you could produce yourself. A further advantage of Lyx is that it handles mathematical formulae rather better than most word processors, so it may be particularly useful for maths and science teachers.

Figure 3.4 The Lyx interface

The philosophy behind document processing is pretty much the opposite to that of desktop publishing. Instead of having greater control over how your document appears you have less – at least while you are writing. However, the output still looks good and you don't have to spend time worrying about appearance. Document processing really comes into its own when you or your learners are producing text-heavy documents or if you are struggling for a way to write non-standard symbols.

Working with PDFs

All the software discussed above – Word, Writer, Scribus and Lyx – can save or export files as PDFs. This function is built into all except Word 2007, which requires a free add-on to be downloaded. PDF files (or portable document format files) can be a little off-putting because they are hard to edit. However, they have multiple advantages over other file formats. PDFs:

- are small files so they are quick to upload and download, and they won't fill up a data stick or your virtual learning environment quickly;

- retain their structure and appearance however many times they are emailed, downloaded and opened on different software and different operating systems (Long and complex word-processed documents are pretty much guaranteed to go wrong under these circumstances!);

- can be annotated but tend to retain their essential information (It is much harder for a mischievous learner to alter a downloaded homework task before passing it on to a friend if it is a PDF!);

- can be read in a browser, meaning that you will never be without the necessary software to open your file, and it is easy to display and distribute your files online.

In order to work with PDFs you will want a good PDF reader and a PDF editor. The industry standard PDF reader is Adobe's Reader. This is freely available for all major operating systems. There are various alternatives around but if you are simply reading PDF documents on a screen and printing them these tend to have few advantages.

The situation becomes a bit more complicated when we decide we want to be able to edit PDFs, however. Recent versions of Adobe Reader have some (at the time of writing very limited) editing tools. For a bit more functionality the best solution will depend on your operating system.

Table 3.3 Key apps: PDF annotation tools

Tool	Platform	Found at	Licence
Foxit Reader	Windows	www.foxitsoftware.com/ Secure_PDF_Reader	Free but not open-source
Skim	Mac	http://skim-app.sourceforge. net	Free & open-source
Xournal	Linux	http://xournal.sourceforge. net	Free & open-source
Foxit mobile	Android & iOS	www.foxitsoftware.com/ products/mobilereader	Free but not open-source

Foxit Reader, Skim and Xournal will allow you to fill in forms, add notes in the margin, highlight key text and draw on a PDF. For a slick commercial alternative consider Adobe's Acrobat Pro. For a good online solution check out PDFescape (www.pdfescape.com). This is a free tool that just requires Internet access.

It is also useful to be able to split multi-page documents and merge pages from PDFs – for example, you might want to make one page from a specification available online, or make up a single revision resource containing past exam papers and their published mark schemes. This requires different tools – again the solutions are specific to your operating system. JPDFTweak works on any operating system; however, it has a less user-friendly interface than the other free tools so I only recommend it as first choice for Mac users seeking a free solution.

Table 3.4 Key apps: PDF split and merge tools

Tool	Platform	Found at	Licence
PDFill Free PDF Tools	Windows	http://www.pdfill.com/ pdf_tools_free.html	Free but not open-source
JPDFTweak (free)	Mac	http://jpdftweak. sourceforge.net	Free & open-source
Acrobat Suite (commercial)		http://www.adobe.com/ products/acrobat.edu. html	Commercial
PDF Mod	Linux	https://live.gnome.org/ PdfMod	Free & open-source
PDF Utility Lite	Android	https://play.google. com/store/apps/ details?id=com.telbyte. lite.pdf&hl=en	Free but not open-source
PDF Splicer	iOS	https://itunes.apple.com/ gb/app/pdf-splicer-free/ id496224447?mt=8	Free but not open-source

Introducing graphics

The technical bit

Locating copyright-free images

The first thing you think about is obtaining suitable images to use in text resources. Most images are protected by copyright, and you aren't supposed to use them. Google image searching is fairly unlikely to find you what you are after. However, images that you are free to use do exist; you just need to know where to look for them. The technical term for pictures that have no copyright issues is *public domain*. Table 3.5 shows a range

of sources of public domain images. There is no abso-
lute guarantee that using these will protect you from all
issues because they may have been incorrectly labelled as
public domain, or they may feature a person or object for
which a fee is levied. However, at the very least, by using
public domain sites you can demonstrate your intention
to comply with the law.

Table 3.5 Sources of public domain images

Title	Web address
Wikimedia Commons	http://commons.wikimedia.org/wiki/ Main_Page
Stock Exchange	http://www.sxc.hu
Flickr Commons	http://flickr.com/commons
MorgueFile	http://www.morguefile.com
Public Domain Pictures	http://www.publicdomainpictures.net
Public Domain Photos	http://www.public-domain-photos.com

When you think images, don't confine yourself to
photographs. Open Clip Art (http://openclipart.org) and
Public Domain Clipart (www.pdclipart.org) provide a very
large set of copyright-free cartoon-type graphics that can
be incorporated into your handouts with no expense and
very little effort. The latter also contains a large collection
of free smileys.

Image-viewing and editing tools

There are a good range of tools around designed to help
you organise and view images that you may want to use
in text resources. Some of these have some basic editing
functions as well; there is always a trade-off between ease
of use and range of features. One tool that achieves a really
good balance here is Google's Picasa.

Working more imaginatively with text

Table 3.6 Key app: Picasa

Publisher	Google	http://picasa.google.com	Licence: Free
Platform	Windows YES	Mac YES	Linux YES
Also consider	DigiKam (all major operating systems), IrfanView (Windows & Linux), iPhoto (Mac)		
Mobile position	Available for Android (free) and iOS (small fee)		

Figure 3.5 The Picasa interface

When you install Picasa it indexes all your files – and backs up images online if you want. Critically, it allows simple editing, so if you just need to crop a picture or remove red-eye this is probably the easiest way to do it. Most of the time, professional quality graphics software is overkill for the busy teacher. Obviously this is different if you teach photography or graphics! If you don't have subject-specific expertise but do find you need something with more power for graphics, there are a couple of options. GIMP (GNU image manipulation programme) is a free but extremely powerful tool. Slightly less sophisticated but much easier to use is Inkscape. GIMP and Inkscape are both free and open-source, and they are available for all major operating systems.

If you want a little more editing power than the very basic image handling tools but are intimidated by something as professional as GIMP, there is a good range of halfway house apps. Many of these are commercial and

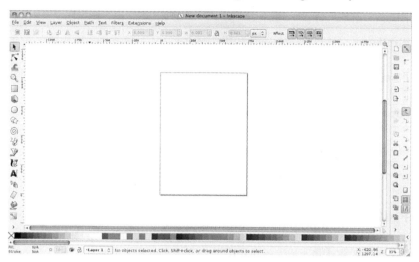

Figure 3.6 The Inkscape interface

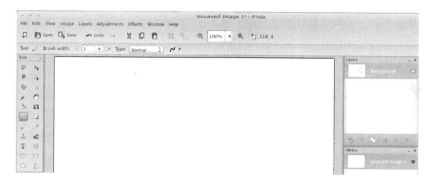

Figure 3.7 The Pinta interface

platform-specific. My personal favourite is Pinta (http://pinta-project.com). This is free and open-source, and available for Windows, Mac and Linux. There is a lot of personal preference to bear in mind when we talk about image editors, but I find Pinta remarkably easy to use.

Working more imaginatively with text

Table 3.7 Key app: Pinta

Publisher	Pinta Project	http://pinta-project.com	Licence: Free & open-source
Platform	Windows YES	Mac YES	Linux YES
Also consider	Paint.NET (Windows) or Seashore (Mac)		
Mobile position	Not available for iOS or Android		

Putting it together in theory and practice

The theory bit

Fonts

Probably more nonsense has probably been written about the use of fonts than any other topic in e-learning. Look on any pop-psychology and education website and you can read about research showing that one font or another is 'easier to read' or 'preferred by learners'. The problem is that research comparing learner responses to different fonts has been bedevilled by 'lurking variables' like default line spacing and character height which differ between fonts. Showing learners different fonts at the same font size and testing which they read fastest, remember best

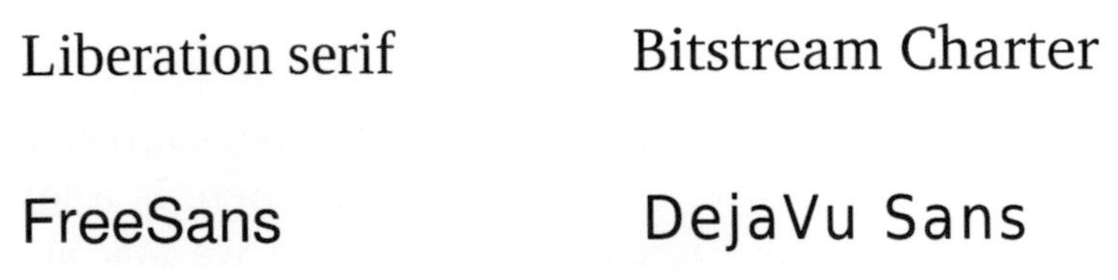

Liberation serif   Bitstream Charter

FreeSans   DejaVu Sans

Figure 3.8 These fonts have been screenshot at the same 'font size'. See how different the sizes actually are

60

or report they can see most simply won't work unless all these variables are controlled.

Comic Sans has come out of font-comparison research quite well; however, this may be largely because at font size 12 its characters are substantially larger than those of the other commonly used fonts, therefore we would expect it to be easier to read. The fact that there are at least two international campaigns dedicated to banning Comic Sans suggests that this is less than the perfect font. A general knee-jerk shift towards using Comic Sans is perhaps another example of the 'cyberlemming' phenomenon.

There is also some suggestion in the research literature that what fonts are easiest to read depends on the context. Sans Serif fonts (more rounded fonts like Arial without long vertical strokes) are often thought of as easier to read, but this may not always be the case in every situation. What is easy to read on screen may not be the same as what is easy on a printed page; what is easy to read in a block of dense text may not be the same as what is easy on a page with plenty of space and images.

Now this is *not* to say that font choice is not important, just that it's worth responding to the preferences of your learners and looking very critically at any 'evidence-based practice' in this area to which you are asked to conform. Check out what your learners like and find easy to work with (these may or may not be the same).

Readability

The physical appearance of a body of text is one thing. However, how easy a body of text is to read also varies in line with several dimensions of the way it is worded. There is a range of formulae around with which a readability index can be calculated. Typically these input variables such as sentence length, number of letters per word and number of syllables per word. For example, the Fog Index is calculated using the following formula:

$$\text{Index} = 0.4 \ (\text{words/sentences} + 100((\text{words} > 2 \text{ syllables/words}))$$

There are interactive websites that will calculate your readability indices for you, but remember that any one readability formula has limited validity. I like readability.info (www.readability.info) because this gives scores using several different readability formulae and also reports on other variables that don't fit neatly into mathematical formulae but which might impact on readability. These include the following:

- Use of the passive voice can make text harder to follow.

- Conjunctions lengthen sentences and may make them harder to follow.

- Too many pronouns can make meaning ambiguous; however, too few tend to lead it to lack fluidity.

Use of textual features

For most teachers the more important element of producing text will be the content. The first thing to consider is our use of text features. To better understand their use I draw on concepts from applied linguistics (after Jarvis, 2011).

- *Coherence features*: involve improving the overall coherence of a passage, for example by adding headings and summaries, and by linking one idea to another.

- *Linking features*: involve explicitly linking new ideas to the reader's existing knowledge. This can be done in the body of text or as a callout.

- *Signalling features*: Key concepts in a piece of text are said to be *signalled* when they are extracted and explained in detail in boxes.

- *Elaboration*: Whenever key terms are defined, irrespective of whether they are signalled, we tend to elaborate on a definition; for example, by paraphrasing it, giving an example or providing a mnemonic device to make it more memorable.

Use of imagery

As discussed in the last chapter, use of imagery appears to make text more friendly and memorable in particular for some learners. We can explain this in various theoretical ways using dual coding theory or the idea of learning styles (see p. 20). A problem with images is copyright. In an educational context the chances of your being caught and punished for any one copyright breach are small but they add up over time! Moreover there are aggressive companies around that make their money by charging schools and colleges to 'vet' their copyright with the threat that if they are not employed they will report the institution to major copyright holders as a likely offender (unless you have been really naughty, just say no). It is therefore worth being aware of sources of copyright-free images – see the next section on practice.

A simple and underused graphic is the smiley! Smileys are a simple way to signal positive and negative responses. They can be used to give graphical form to emotional or more analytical responses to stimuli. Take the example in Figure 3.9. This signals a more analytical view, and is

Figure 3.9 A smiley suitable for signalling a negative evaluation point (from www.pdclipart.org)

suitable for critiquing a theory or an example of bad practice in a more practical subject.

Use of structural graphics

Often we can enhance a document by including some sort of graphical information. These might include flow diagrams, pie-charts, small mind maps or concept maps. MS Word has included SmartArt since 2007. SmartArt includes a wide range of structural graphics you can use to make information more accessible, in particular to students who prefer working with imagery rather than dense text. A simple way to include SmartArt in handouts is to use something like the Vertical Chevrons feature to define objectives or learning outcomes for a piece of work.

Now there is a note of caution to be sounded here. If you are going to make your handouts available in a range of user-friendly formats (this is discussed in detail on p. 140) SmartArt may not be the way to go. It won't, for example, play nicely with e-book formats, and you can't easily

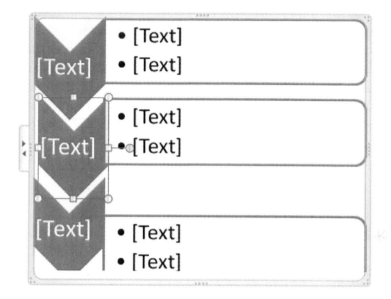

Figure 3.10 Vertical Chevrons are useful for learning outcomes

translate contents into formats more friendly to visually impaired learners. If you are just planning on giving paper resources, however, or making them available in standard document formats on a VLE (see p. 103) then you may find that SmartArt enhances their appeal significantly.

Interactive elements

Think back to our principles of effective learning discussed in Chapter 1. Effective learning is active, interactive, memorable and salient to the learner. Introducing interactive exercises to written documents can help with all of these. Engaging with a task is active, and some exercises can require collaboration, introducing interactivity. The mental effort required to answer questions and consider issues is probably greater than that required to simply read a page, therefore material is likely to be deeply processed and better remembered. Exercises can be devised that increase the personal salience of the subject matter. In fact these elements are so intrinsic to any text resource that the distinction between 'handout' and 'worksheet' is largely redundant; any text resource should require work regardless of whether it contains a body of information. There is little or no place now for a 'handout' in the old sense of a text-heavy non-interactive resource.

The practice

Compare the two documents shown in Figure 3.11 and apply the theoretical understanding shown above. The first page is traditional and the second more modern.

Ignore any content you can make out on these pages. The point is the visual impression they make and the way information is structured. There are a number of key differences here, some obvious and some a little more subtle. The second page

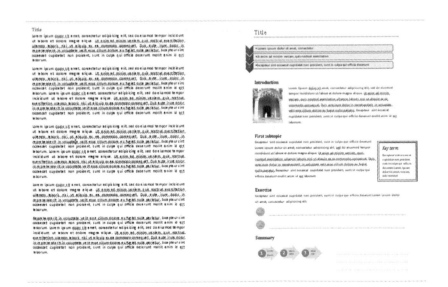

Figure 3.11 A traditional and modern text resource

has a lot more visible white space, including between lines and between paragraphs. It has graphics in the form of a photograph, SmartArt and smileys. It has less text, but opportunities for learner engagement. In spite of the obvious difference in wordage, the difference in the volume of information conveyed in the two pages may be rather less than first appears once the interactive exercises are completed. The second page has visible coherence features in the form of learning objectives, subtitles and summary. There is also signalling in the form of the 'key term' box. In case there is any doubt, the second page represents the way to go! I have included a checklist (Table 3.8) to help reflect on the quality of text resources.

Conclusions and reflections

The handout (at least in the traditional sense of a text-heavy, non-interactive document) is largely dead. This

Table 3.8 Checklist for text documents

	Issue	Check	
1	Overall, is there the right amount of information on a page?	Yes [ ]	No [ ]
2	Is there sufficient space between lines and/or paragraphs?	Yes [ ]	No [ ]
3	Have images/graphics been used as appropriate?	Yes [ ]	No [ ]
4	Is the text sufficiently readable for the age and ability group?	Yes [ ]	No [ ]
5	Are there enough coherence features, e.g. objectives, bullets, numbers, SmartArt?	Yes [ ]	No [ ]
6	Is key information signalled appropriately, e.g. definition box?	Yes [ ]	No [ ]
7	Are key concepts elaborated?	Yes [ ]	No [ ]
8	Are key concepts linked to existing knowledge?	Yes [ ]	No [ ]
9	Are there exercises that require the learner to think?	Yes [ ]	No [ ]

is not the same as saying that our learners should never be exposed to such documents, of course. We don't do future undergrads any favours by ensuring they never see anything that looks like a journal article prior to university. However, teacher-generated resources should generally be friendlier to diverse learners. The interactive text resource is now king! In a media-rich cultural environment it is important that our text resources live up to the standards learners have come to expect. A modern text resource should be visually attractive and easy to follow, with thought given to space, coherence features, graphics, signalling and, most important, an element of interactivity. It should use age-appropriate language.

There is any number of tools with which to generate text resources. Some may be well suited to particular purposes though so it's worth having at least a passing familiarity with a range, including desktop publishing as well as word processing applications. I would also seriously consider – if you haven't already – publishing in PDF format, although to work effectively with PDFs there are a further couple of apps to get your head around. It is also worth familiarising yourself with some graphics tools. Most of us won't need to master anything too advanced here, and you'll be reasonably well placed just using Picasa and Pinta. Remember to think laterally around graphics. SmartArt, smileys and clip art can, when used right, enhance a document as well as photographs.

CHAPTER 4

Introducing multimedia

By the end of this chapter you should be able to:

- appreciate the potential of multimedia to enhance learner experiences;
- understand reasons and ways to present information in auditory form using tools like Audacity and Zamzar, and consider the usefulness of podcasting;
- consider how to present and generate video material, with particular reference to the use of YouTube, VLC and CamStudio;
- consider pedagogical strategies for using video including presentation, screencasting, vodcasting and learner-led filming;
- consider a possible role for both teacher and learner-led animation.

What is multimedia?

Multimedia can be defined as 'multiple forms of media (text, graphics, images, animation, audio and video) that work together' (Eskicioglu and Kopec, 2003). It can thus be pretty much anything that you can see or hear, and at the time of writing there are moves afoot to bring the experience of smell to computers! Chapters 2 and 3 deal with text and graphics, and in practice when e-learning folks talk about multimedia we are almost always referring to the use of sound and video to enhance the learner experience. There are several reasons why it can be a good plan to involve this kind of multimedia in your teaching:

- To deliver information efficiently. Although philosophically most of us don't see education in terms of content delivery, thinking pragmatically, if your learners are taking a course with public exams they will need to know a body of content. Using sound and in particular video can help make material both more comprehensible and memorable.

- To increase congruence between learners' experiences of your teaching and their experiences outside education. Most of our learners use technology to regularly access a range of media in a range of contexts, and so they are likely to be very comfortable with education delivered this way – and remember that even if this involves tech that you are relatively unfamiliar with, it will be what your learners are expecting.

- To cater for individual cognitive differences. The idea that learners neatly divide up into the visual, the verbal, the kinaesthetic, etc., is pretty much discredited nowadays, however the existence of styles of learning is a truism. Different people learn most effectively in different ways, and communicating using a range of media may well help you reach a wider range of learners.

- To keep planning a creative and motivating process for the teacher. This may sound a bit like the tail wagging the dog, but as teachers it is easy to get stale. Introducing some new creative thinking and exciting new ICT in the form of multimedia to the planning process is, for some of us at least, an effective way of staying fresh and motivated.

- To make assessment a more creative and motivating process for your learners. To teachers of media and the creative arts it will be second nature to make assessments as creative as possible, but the rest of us can probably learn a few tricks here. Of course whatever your subject you will want to tailor the nature of your formative assessments to the final assessment. However, within this there is some wriggle-room, and it may be possible to assess students working on multimedia projects.

Working with sound

The technical bit

The 'industry standard' software for sound recording is Audacity. This is a free and open-source tool that can you can use to record from a microphone or from your operating system, meaning that you can record any sound playing on the computer. Audacity is comprehensive and complex, and it does far more than you would ever need to know about in the classroom (unless of course you are a music teacher!) However, to record yourself or your learners speaking using Audacity is quite straightforward. Just plug in a microphone and hit the red button. The only slight complication to get used to when new to Audacity is that by default you save output as an Audacity file, so to keep a file in a standard audio format like MP3 you need to hit 'export' in the file menu.

Table 4.1 Key app: Audacity

Publisher	SourceForge	http://audacity. sourceforge. net/	Licence: Free & open-source
Platform	Windows YES	Mac YES	Linux YES
Also consider	Myna (online), Jokosher (Windows & Linux), Ardour (Mac & Linux)		
Mobile position	Available on iOS and Android (requires Linux installer app)		

A brief word about sound file formats

If you are going to deal with sound you need to know a little bit about file formats. When possible I tend to keep sound files as MP3s. An MP3 is a compressed sound file. By 'compressed' I mean that it has been reduced in size by removing some information that makes minimal difference to the experience of the listener. MP3s are quite small files, meaning they are easy to store or to send by e-mail. They can be played on a wide variety of media players including mobile devices like iPods.

For most purposes MP3s will be of sufficient quality, but there are times when quality is paramount such as if you are broadcasting over a PA in the school hall. For this you might prefer a lossless format like WAV. WAV files are much larger than MP3s, but the sound quality is better. Although the WAV format is owned by Microsoft you should be able to play WAVs on any operating system (though not on all portable MP3 players, so beware!)

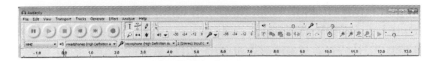

Figure 4.1 The Audacity interface

There are situations where you want to convert an existing text document to an audio format like MP3. Audacity on its own won't help you here. Online file conversion sites like Zamzar (www.zamzar.com) do a very good job of this type of conversion. If you are a Windows user and you prefer a downloaded app to working online try Dimio D-Speech or Clipspeak. Mac and Linux operating systems have built-in text-to-speech engines, so you can convert a document to MP3 by simply activating the screen reader and recording the output using Audacity.

The theory bit

There is a range of theoretical reasons why students might make good use of audio files. Perhaps the most basic reason is that short-term memory has auditory and visual channels, and learners may find it easier to process information if they swap between visual and auditory modes. This means that learners who alternate between reading and listening to audio files are likely to remember more, or at least be able to concentrate for longer than those who simply read.

There are of course individual differences between learners, and this won't work for everyone. Some teachers like to think of individual cognitive differences in terms of learning styles. Some common systems for classifying learning style make reference to *auditory learners*, individuals with a preference for listening to information. The theoretical basis for this type of classification is very weak and classification tools have very poor validity (Coffield et al., 2004), so I wouldn't recommend pushing audio files on particular students just because your school or college has classified them as 'auditory'. On the other hand (whether we call this learning style or not) it is likely that some of your learners will be particularly at home with information in auditory form. Using a tool like Audacity or Zamzar it is straightforward to make information available in audio format.

Audio files should also be helpful to students with visual impairment and may also be of use for individuals with specific learning difficulties like dyslexia. Although dyslexia typically involves some degree of difficulty in processing verbal information in auditory as well as visual channels, at least some learners with dyslexia find it easier to process verbal information in auditory form than visual. Studies (such as that by Diraa et al., 2009) have found that assistive technology that presents text documents in auditory form has a moderate positive impact on learning.

The practice

So we know a little bit about how to work with sound files and we have a theoretical basis for wanting to. Perhaps the least obvious aspect of this is actually how to incorporate audio in teaching. In most teaching contexts we would expect to find that learners won't respond particularly well to being asked to sit for very long or very often in class listening to the spoken word. Without even the non-verbal communication that accompanies a live speaker, there will be little to engage learners.

There are things you can do with sound though. One simple strategy is to populate a virtual learning environment with audio versions of key documents so that learners have a choice in what form they access learning materials. Some learners may opt for audio versions to suit their information processing style, and others will make more pragmatic decisions; for example, those with a long car or bus journey to and from school or college would find it impractical to use this time to read, but they might well be able to listen to their handouts on a portable audio device like an iPod.

Figure 4.2 Learners probably won't read notes on a long bus journey home but they might listen to an MP3

One way to make the sharing of audio files more congruent with the use of technology outside education is to podcast. A podcast is a feed to a website containing audio files to which users subscribe. The advantage of this over simply posting MP3s online is that the content automatically updates for the user. That may all sound a bit complicated, but the practice of podcasting is made very simple by online services.

I particularly like Podbean (www.podbean.com). With Podbean you produce an *episode*, which contains text and an audio (or video) file. You then simply invite users to subscribe (normally by e-mail). You can embed Podbean in your virtual learning environment and users can subscribe using their Smartphones or desktops. Once subscribed there is no awkward transfer of files between devices – content simply appears on the phone. An alternative is to podcast using iTunes. This is a slightly more fiddly process and you don't have as many options, but there is no getting away from the fact that iTunes has a lot of street-cred, and your learners will enjoy using it (and probably think you are rather cool).

Podcasting does not have to be teacher-led. Producing podcasts is often within the technological abilities of learners, and you will probably find that a project that will be shared on iTunes will be much more motivating to many learners than another word-processed essay. Remember that learner engagement and enthusiasm are central to the current Ofsted framework, and that project work with a podcast outcome is likely to fulfil these criteria. Remember as well that putting audio material online can be personal or for sharing. There are now multimedia blogging sites (like Tumblr), that really benefit learners who like to keep a reflective blog of their learning but who don't want to be limited to textual records.

Working with video

The technical bit

The first thing you need is a decent media player. One of the common disaster-scenarios that has put many teachers off using technology in the classroom in the past is the one where a video file that plays fine in one classroom fails completely in another where there is a different media player. There are two main reasons for this:

- *File type and codec*: video files come in a number of formats. The most common media players don't play the full range of file types, so you can be unlucky and end up with a media file that won't play on your media player. Video files have a code-decode system (or codec for short). This means that they will only play on systems that have a licence to decode and play the file. A change of media player can mean you are using something not licensed to decode your file.

- *Default media settings*: every machine in your school or college will have a default media player. This may be set centrally or alternatively it might have been set manually on every machine. If you know what media player you want to use to open a file don't just double click on the file – that will open it with the default media player. Right click and select 'open with' the software you know will work.

Everyone has their personal favourites when it comes to media players, but personally I would steer clear of some of those most commonly found in schools (I'm not going to name them and risk law suits). There are two media players that stand out a mile for supporting an outstanding range of formats and codecs. These are VLC and MPlayer. VLC is a particularly useful tool because of its range of functionality, but MPlayer is reportedly even more versatile when it comes to playing unusual file types. VLC (confusingly) stands for video local area network client. Ignore this though – VLC is just a very good media player.

VLC will play DVDs, downloaded YouTube clips and almost any media file. It is also a useful tool to record from a webcam, which means you can easily extend the idea of podcasting to include vodcasting (podcasting video material).

Table 4.2 Key app: VLC

Publisher	VideoLAN Organisation	www.videolan. org	Licence: Free & open-source
Platform	Windows YES	Mac YES	Linux YES
Also consider	MPlayer (very wide range of codecs but fewer advanced features than VLC)		
Mobile position	Available on both iOS and Android		

Introducing multimedia

Figure 4.3 The VLC interface

YouTube

Although VLC is an excellent media player, there are a couple of other tools you will need to master to get the most out of working with video. YouTube and its clones are an excellent source of a massive range of video material (you can see a selection of video-sharing sites in Table 4.3). If your school or college allows access that's really handy because some of the best uses of YouTube in the classroom are spontaneous rather than planned – a learner brings a suggestion for a video source or something comes up in discussion that cries out for a video explanation. However, whether you can access YouTube from work or not I would strongly recommend a download tool so that you can keep particularly good YouTube videos (many of the best tend to be removed periodically).

The easiest way to download online videos such as from YouTube is with a browser add-on. Firefox is generally the best browser for add-ons (see p. 98 for a more detailed

Table 4.3 A selection of video-sharing sites

Site	URL	Special features
YouTube	www.youtube.com	Probably the largest video sharing site
DailyMotion	www.dailymotion.com	Very similar to Youtube
Vimeo	https://vimeo .com	Good for more arty videos
VideoJug	www.videojug.com	Specifically for 'how to' videos
WatchKnow Learn	www.watchknowlearn.org	Specifically for education, categorised by subject

78

discussion). I use Flash Video Downloader (www.flash-videodownloader.org) but there are plenty of similar tools around. Alternatively you can watch YouTube through VLC; just open 'network' on the media menu and paste in the web address of the online video. You can record any video played in VLC – see the section below on video editing.

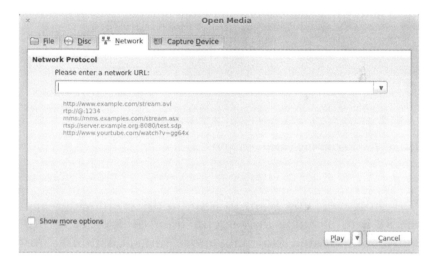

Figure 4.4 You can stream online video through VLC and record it if you wish

Video editing tools

You can perform some very simple video editing with VLC (at the time of writing this does not apply to Mac users unfortunately). Often all you want to do is extract a short segment from a DVD or YouTube download. You can do this using VLC's advanced menu. This is not visible by default but you can activate it on the view menu – see Figure 4.5.

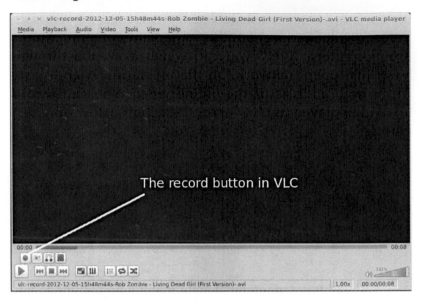

Figure 4.5 Recording video using VLC

If, however, you want to join up different video segments into a single longer clip then things get a little more complicated and a lot more time-consuming. My advice is therefore to do this relatively infrequently. You will need a proper video editor, and these are a little more complicated to use. The major standard and (relatively) straightforward video editing tools are platform-specific.

Moviemaker, iMovie and Openshot have a very similar interface. Essentially you add video clips to a project, then drag them on to a timeline, so that they play one after the other. This can get a bit fiddly, especially when you start to add in transitions between each clip. I would always look carefully at what you want to achieve with a film and consider whether the extra effort involved in video editing is justified.

Table 4.4 Key apps: video editing tools

Tool	Platform	Found at	Licence
Movie-Maker	Windows	http://windows.microsoft.com/en-US/windows7/products/features/movie-maker	Commercial
iMovie	Mac	http://www.apple.com/ilife/imovie	Commercial
Openshot	Linux	www.openshot.org	Free & open-source
Androvid	Android	https://play.google.com/store/apps/details?id=com.androvid&hl=en_GB	Free and pro versions
Magisto	iOS	https://itunes.apple.com/gb/app/magisto-magical-video-editor/id486781045?mt=8	Free but not open-source

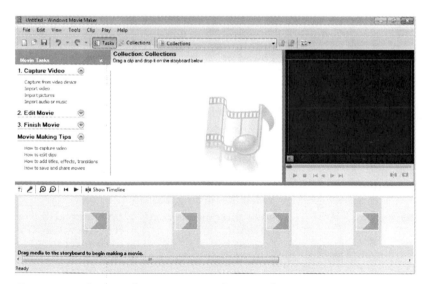

Figure 4.6 The Windows Movie Maker interface

Screencasting tools

Screencasting involves recording whatever is happening on a desktop and saving it as a video file. This is particularly useful when giving learners instruction in how to carry out a task involving the computer. Screencast tools tend to be platform-specific, and vary enormously in price. There are several perfectly adequate free tools available for all the major operating systems (though Mac users will find yourselves more limited than others), but you can pay several hundred pounds for top-end products. Look for the following features in a good screencast tool:

- records sound as well as video so you can narrate a screencast;

- saves in an easy-to-use video format;

- records the whole screen or a selected area.

Table 4.5 Key apps: screencast tools

Tool	Platform	Found at	Licence
Camstudio	Windows	http://camstudio.org	Free & open-source
Jing	Mac	http://www.techsmith. com/jing.html	Free version records up to 5 minutes
XVidCap	Linux	http://xvidcap. sourceforge.net	Free & open-source
Full HD Video Recorder	Android	https://play.google. com/store/apps/ details?id=com.Full_HD_ Video_Recording_206263	Free. No licence information available
Reflector	iOS	www.airsquirrels.com/ reflector	Commercial and requires a Mac OS to connect to

An alternative to these desktop tools is Screencast-o-matic (www.screencast-o-matic.com/screen_recorder). This is an online application that downloads an applet (an applet is simply a small programme) that carries out the recording. There are a couple of technical provisos with this option – you have to be online, you need up-to-date Java and the Internet

Figure 4.7 The CamStudio interface

Figure 4.8 The Screencast-o-matic applet

security settings in your school or college may prevent the applet downloading or running – but the recording quality is very good so it's worth having a go. Note that at the time of writing SOM does not work on mobile operating systems.

The theory bit

E-learning specialists often talk about breaking the PowerPoint 'glass ceiling'. By this we mean that many teachers master PowerPoint but do not take their ICT to the next level. The term is particularly applicable when we talk about video-based multimedia because in using this kind of multimedia we are consciously pushing the boundaries of how and what visual information we can present on a screen. As Eskicioglu and Kopec (2003) say, [video-based] multimedia is 'unparalleled in its ability to disseminate information quickly and accurately' (p. 1).

All the theoretical reasons for using audio are true for using video. Information from a video is processed in auditory and visual channels, meaning that we can probably pick up more information in a given time. Incidentally, always be suspicious of statistics saying that we remember X per cent of what we hear or read, Y per cent of what we see and Z per cent of what we do! These figures are bandied about as if they were undisputed fact, but actually recall will vary wildly according to the material, the learner and the context. However, it is probably true that the integration of visual and auditory content in video makes material easier to understand and remember.

Given the omnipresence of video material in every other aspect of learners' lives it is also likely that using video in and around the classroom helps make learning congruent with learners' everyday experience. However, we have to adapt our practice accordingly. I find that a spontaneous YouTube search in response to a learner's question often works very well, mostly because it is how the class would have solved the problem if I hadn't been there – YouTube, like Wikipedia, is an established cultural tool for problem-solving.

Figure 4.9 YouTube is an important cultural tool for problem-solving and informal learning

The practice

We can't simply convert documents to video like we can audio, so we have to give the source of our video material a bit of thought. When we select a video we have the choice of using an existing one, taking clips from it or creating one from scratch. To flesh that out a bit here are some options:

- Show DVDs in full or part. Depending on the context these could be documentaries, bespoke education resources or entertainment media.

- Download footage from video-sharing sites like YouTube, and show it in full, create a shorter clip using VLC or combine clips into a new video using video editing software.

- Make a screencast of whatever is happening on screen.

- Record a video using a video camera or webcam.

Video as stimulus material

A video can be used as a stimulus to generate discussion. Often the shorter, more dramatic and more ambiguous it is the better. Remember the aim here is not to put across information but to arouse interest in a topic and get learners engaged and thinking. Remember as well that although this type of 'fascinator' works well as a starter activity, we can have a 'starter' any time we introduce a new idea; it doesn't have to be at the beginning of a lesson. A clip from popular culture such as a TV series or film works well, although it can be very helpful to cue learners in with a task before they watch – this makes it easier to steer the conversation away from the film or series itself on to what you had in mind to discuss. Also bear in mind that in the current Ofsted framework, progress in learning has to be visible at whatever time an observer visits a lesson – this is hard to evidence if learners are watching a film for the duration of a visit! Think short and focused, and be clear what you are asking learners to *do* with the video.

Video as a medium for putting across information

This is the most obvious use of video in the classroom. However, it is also tricky because there is a potential conflict between the ability of video to put across complex ideas efficiently and the ideal of student-centred learning – which is of course now enshrined in policy. Traditionally, many of us have used extended video as much to pace ourselves in a hectic day as to optimise learning. Times change though and anything that looks suspiciously like you planned it in order to put your feet up for a bit is not going to cut it in the current regime. Don't throw out the baby with the bathwater though; try the following:

- Use VLC to cut segments from the film. This way you are separating out individual ideas that can each form the basis of an activity. Because you are just picking out the key moments in the video the total time needed to work through the material need not differ much from what you would have spent passively watching the video in its entirety. The point is that learners are active throughout.

- Make sure learners know why they are watching each clip – perhaps link it back to an objective. Follow it with a student-centred activity and check learning. For added spice, change pairs or groups around for each activity. If the content of the video builds towards a larger idea you can match this with a 'snowball' of small groups feeding into larger groups at each stage of the activity.

Screencasting

Using a tool like CamStudio it is technologically very straightforward to record a desktop. You can use this as a way to keep task instructions available for learners as they work independently – particularly outside lesson time. This comes into its own if learners are required to do something different from what they are used to, perhaps with unfamiliar or unfriendly technology. Also consider the possibility of learners screencasting their activity and this forming the basis of an assessment. Where you want to assess an activity with an uncertain outcome – such as an Internet search task – a record of the process the learner went through may actually be a more valid measure of success than the outcome, i.e. what they found.

Vodcasting

This awkward term is simply a contraction of 'video' and 'podcasting'. Rather than just recording an audio message for learners try filming yourself using a webcam and posting that. The easiest way to record a vodcast is through VLC. Just go to the Media menu and select 'Open capture device'. If you are using a built-in webcam (which most laptops now have) you needn't select anything, just click 'okay'. When you are ready to record just hit the red record button on the advanced tools menu.

Like screencasting you can pass vodcasting over to your learners, who can for example produce peer revision resources or pass on advice to the next cohort on a course.

Figure 4.10 A vodcast recorded in VLC. Watch the angle of your webcam or your chin may end up enlarged on screen!

Figure 4.11 Fieldwork can be enhanced by filming

Learner-led filming

How useful it is to let your learners loose with video cameras probably depends on your subject, although never underestimate the creativity some teachers bring to their planning! In a media or technology-oriented subject there is a clear rationale for student filming; you might have to use a bit more imagination to build filming into a maths lesson – although I don't doubt it can be done. Any subject that includes fieldwork can benefit from a video record and any social science can make use of recorded interviews. Don't forget that many of your learners will have Smartphones that can record video – you don't have to think in terms of major expenditure or learning to use complicated new hardware.

Working with animation

Animation involves stringing together a sequence of static images, generally so that they appear to move. Some but by no means all animation is interactive, so you can influence what happens during an animated sequence as well as simply playing it. At its simplest, animation can merely involve making slide shows of related images but without the illusion of movement. This may then be overlaid with a soundtrack either narrating the portrayed scene or simulating a dialogue between characters in the scene. Animation can make a big visual impact but it can take hours to produce an animation lasting a few seconds, so we should think very carefully about how to resource animations and when it is a good use of time.

The technical bit

There are three ways to obtain an animation:

- *Use existing animations.* Depending on your level and subject there is quite a good chance you will find existing relevant animations for your teaching. These may be publically available, for example on YouTube, or commercially available as part of subject software packages. Some organisations such as the Wellcome Trust provide freely a range of very good quality animations for science teaching. Using existing animations may or may not involve a direct cost, but if suitable animations are available this may be the most efficient use of time. The downside is that you are unlikely to get the precise animation you would have liked had you designed it yourself.

- *Produce your own animations.* There are various pieces of software and specialist websites that allow you to produce animations of varying complexity. Some of these are free. The upside to working this way is that you can control the end result, at least within the limits of your expertise. The downside is the tremendous investment of time required, both to master animation apps and to produce the animations themselves. If you enjoy this process then go for it, but animation production is a creative specialism in its own right; don't feel that it is a basic competency of being a teacher!

- *Get your learners to produce them.* This is very consuming of lesson time, but it is potentially very engaging for learners. Whether it is a good use of time depends on your circumstances. If you are looking for efficient transfer of information prior to an exam this probably isn't the way to go, but if you are more concerned with your learners exploring a topic over time and acquiring a transferable skill into the bargain, this may be the way to go.

Table 4.6 Key apps: animation tools

Tool	Platform	Found at	Description	Licence
Animoto	Online	http://animoto.com	Allows simple animations using existing templates	Free lite version
Pencil	Windows, Mac, Linux	http://www.pencil-animation.org	Allows animation of line drawings	Free & open-source
Blender	Windows, Mac, Linux	www.blender.org	An advanced professional tool for a range of animations	Free & open-source
Animation Desk	Windows, Mac, iOS, Android	www.kdanmobile.com/en/products.html		Free for Android. Commercial licence. Paid on other platforms

Introducing multimedia

If you or your learners are going to produce animations you need an appropriate app. There are many of these around and you may have a site licence and in-house expertise for one or more of the higher-end commercial options. In the following key apps box I just introduce three free options.

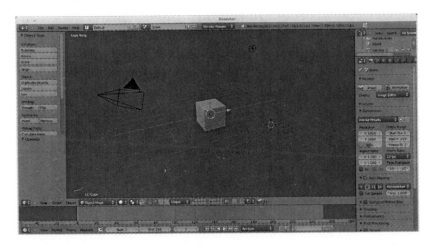

Figure 4.12 The Blender interface

The theory and practice

Animation provides an interesting lens to look at the distinction between constructivist and transmission models of learning. As teachers we can either use animations ourselves to efficiently put across information, or we can hand the responsibility over to our learners and let them do the work. Bertrancourt (2005) suggests three ways in which animation can be used to enhance learning:

- Animation can be used to enhance learners' visual representations of a phenomenon, like a static image but better.

- Animation can be used to illustrate processes that already occur but which may be hard to see, such as the relative speed at which objects of different weight fall.

- Where an animation has an interactive element – this can be as simple as a pause button – it can be the basis of hypothesis testing, perhaps as part of a 'what happens next' discussion.

It is equally interesting to look at animation from the perspective of quality assurance. The PTBs will use exam results as key performance indicators, and in terms of exam preparation in most subjects animation is likely to be used as an efficient means of transmission. However, there is a disconnect between what works in exam preparation and what observers emulating the Ofsted inspection framework wish to see, and for lesson observation purposes learner-led animation is the way to go.

You can see that there are practical, theoretical and quality issues to consider here, and most teachers will probably not wish to make much use of animation except where suitable animations already exist and can be used as an alternative to static images or video. I would recommend a good search for such animations in your subject, however. They may now and again be the key to getting across a tricky concept.

Conclusions and reflections

There are many good reasons for being more imaginative with the media we use to communicate ideas to learners and with which we equip them to communicate thereafter. On a cognitive level, using sound and video should enhance the quality of information processing and hence learning. On a cultural level, multimedia makes formal learning more congruent with the everyday experiences of learners – including informal learning.

There is no shortage of free and low-cost software with which to play, edit, record and distribute multimedia, and much if not all of this is surprisingly straightforward to use. The exception here is perhaps animation, and although animation can really enhance a lesson, I would think carefully about the time needed for you or your learners to produce it. The trickier issues are around using multimedia in ways that actually enhance learning and are compatible with the current quality assurance context. I have offered some suggestions but I feel strongly that we shouldn't be too prescriptive here – multimedia and creativity go hand in hand and individual teachers will quite rightly run with their own ideas and develop their own strategies.

CHAPTER 5

Taking learning online

By the end of this chapter you should be able to:

- appreciate the potential of the Internet for learning and know about the basics of Internet access;
- be familiar with some of the issues around Internet searching and select tools and design tasks appropriate for your learners;
- create custom search engines and webquests;
- design and use a virtual learning environment (VLE) with particular reference to Moodle;
- produce online lessons with particular reference to Blendspace;
- know about online back-up tools and equip learners with an e-Portfolio using Mahara;
- understand what is meant by Web2.0 and incorporate blogs, wikis, forums and social networks into your teaching;
- mash up a range of online tools into a single interface using NetVibes.

Of all the chapters in this book this is perhaps the one that moves fastest from the everyday to the quite radical, so be warned! By 'radical' I mean both that I am proposing some technology that will be unfamiliar to most people and, more importantly, some non-traditional ways of working with learners. Let's start with the basics of using the Internet though.

The Web as a searchable resource

The technical bit

The Internet (which technically should be capitalised as a noun but not when used as an adjective) is a world-wide system of interconnected computer networks. The Internet allows us to access the World Wide Web, which is the collective term for all the resources that are available via the Internet. Originally the Internet and World Wide Web were the province of highly technical users, mostly scientists who used it to share data. Two particular pieces of technology have facilitated effective use of the Internet for us ordinary folks:

- *The browser*: this is a piece of desktop software that allows us to easily navigate from one part of the Internet to another by means of identifying a particular web resource by its URL (or uniform resource locator).

- *The search engine*: without some way of locating what we are looking for online we could only navigate the Internet by knowing the precise URL of every resource. This would be a painfully slow and clumsy process. Search engines like Google make it possible to find resources that are likely to meet your requirements through input of key words.

Choosing your browser(s)

The main piece of software you need to do anything online is a browser. If you buy a Windows computer anywhere in

Europe you are currently presented with a choice of browsers. This is the result of a decision at European level that shipping computers with just Microsoft's own Internet Explorer breached competition law and was unfair to those producing rival browser products. But enough of Geek Politique, you are probably more interested in what works. Actually, you need more than one browser to be sure of using the Internet effectively. There are many browsers around, and they all have their strengths and weaknesses, but I recommend these three for particular reasons:

- *Internet Explorer (IE)* (produced by Microsoft): this is the browser most commonly used worldwide, but largely because in most countries it is the only browser shipped with Windows computers. ICT and e-learning professionals tend to be quite sniffy about IE, but (if you are using Windows) you do need it simply because it interacts with websites rather differently from other browsers and you will come across some sites that only work well in IE. However, you will also find sites that don't work well in IE so you need at least one other weapon in your browser arsenal.

- *Firefox* (produced by the Mozilla Corporation): this is a very good general browser that has the particular advantage of an enormous range of add-ons. Add-ons are extra functions that can be downloaded and switched on in the browser. You can, for example, download online video using an add-on. At the time of writing Firefox has by far the largest selection of add-ons.

Figure 5.1 The Internet Explorer interface

Figure 5.2 The Firefox interface

- *Chrome*: produced by Google, this is the 'new kid on the block' but in some ways the best browser around. New versions of all the major browsers are being published every few months so this may change, but at the time of writing Chrome is the fastest of the major browsers. It is also the most flexible in operating online media that require plug-ins like Flash and Java. Ever had the frustrating experience of going to demonstrate something on a website during a lesson and receiving a message onscreen saying that it won't play because X or Y is not up to date? Where possible, Chrome gives you the option of running the application with an out-of-date plug-in.

Figure 5.3 The Chrome interface

With a bit of fiddling you can probably make any of these browsers run on any operating system, but by default Macs come with Safari instead of Internet Explorer. Internet Explorer is only supported by Microsoft for Windows and neither Safari nor IE are officially supported on Linux.

Mobile platforms use a similar range of browsers, thus you will find Safari as the default browser on an iPad. Others can be installed, however. Mobile browsers won't currently give you quite the same experience as desktop browsers. They won't run Java applets, and will have a smaller range of add-ons. Always check whether your favourite sites work in a mobile browser before using it in class with learners' phones or the class set of tablets. It may be that non-mobile friendly sites provide an app you can use instead.

Search tools

There are many ways to search for material online, but to most of us searching is synonymous with the Google search engine. Google deserve enormous credit for producing the first search engine to really work, and for most general purposes it is still probably the best tool. However, there are other ways to go.

- *Existing subject-specific search tools*: these exist for many subjects and range in level from dictionaries to professional-level search engines and databases. Check out some examples in the practice section on p. 102.

- *Custom search engines*: using Google technology you can create your own search engine that will search just the sites you select in advance.

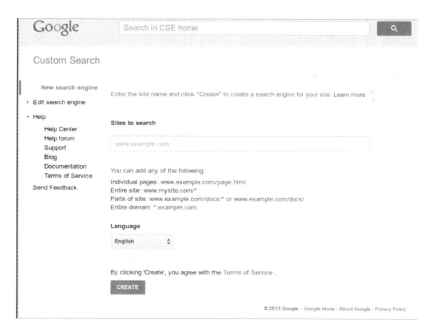

Figure 5.4 Creating a custom Google search engine

Now, as you might expect, creating your own search engine is slightly more technical and fiddly than most of the ICT tasks described in this book. However, Google have done the really hard bit for you. You will need access to your own web page – your school or college should be able to provide this. You also need to create a Google account if you don't have one already. When you are logged in to Google, find the *custom search* link. Give your custom engine a name and description and list the web addresses of the sites you'd like it to search. Google will then generate the necessary computer code. Save this and paste it into the body of the html view of your web page. That's it!

The theory bit

The Internet provides an unprecedented opportunity for learners to take control of their learning and work independently. This very much captures the sort of active and independent learning we should be requiring from our learners. Browsers and search engines have provided an unprecedented opportunity for students to explore the world, asking their own questions and seeking their own sources of information (Churach and Fisher, 2001). On the other hand, unless you set tasks up carefully, most exploration using the Net tends to be quite superficial (Selinger, 2001), with learners tending to locate and re-present existing materials rather than making the decisions and following lines of enquiry that would make searching a really active task.

Search tasks thus benefit from being well thought out in advance and from teacher scaffolding while they are carried out. Dodge (1995) has suggested a model for making sure learning is active, and that learners understand why they are carrying out the task. This is explored in the practice section (p. 102).

Figure 5.5 Learners can be more independent learners through
Internet searching

The practice

Using subject dictionaries

We need to give some thought to level and also to differentiation. For more independent A-level students something quite advanced might be the way to go; however, for many learners it will be more productive to introduce them to online subject dictionaries. Remember that students are likely to be working fairly independently on search tasks so they may need a source of basics like a dictionary if they are not to find themselves stuck. Examples of subject dictionaries are shown in Table 5.1.

Using subject search engines

Table 5.2 shows a range of subject-specific search tools. Some sites that use the term 'search engine' are true search engines in the sense that they search the Internet, whilst

Table 5.1 Examples of subject-specific dictionaries

Subject	Site name	Web address
Maths	Maths is fun	www.mathsisfun.com/definitions/index.html
Biology	BiologyOnline	www.biology-online.org/dictionary/Main_Page
Chemistry	Chemicool	www.chemicool.com/dictionary.html
Geography	GeographyDictionary	www.geography-dictionary.org
History	Babylon.com	www.babylon.com/define/52/History-Dictionary.html
Psychology	AllPsych	http://allpsych.com/dictionary

Table 5.2 Examples of subject-specific search engines

Subject	Site name	Web address
Maths	Maths Class	http://mathsclass.net/comments/mathsclass-search-engine
Biology	Bio Explorer	www.bioexplorer.net/Search_Engines
Chemistry	Chemistry Guide	www.chemistryguide.org
Geography	Geo Interactive	www.geointeractive.co.uk/gse.htm
History	Buscopio	www.buscopio.net/eng/index.php?cat=536
Psychology	Psych Spider	www.zpid.de/PsychSpider.php?lang=EN

others are technically online databases; however, learners' experience of using them is quite similar. This certainly isn't meant to be an exhaustive list and as a subject specialist you may well know of better tools, but it does illustrate the existence of search tools other than generic Google.

Webquesting: A way to ensure searching leads to learning

One approach to structuring search tasks is the webquest (Dodge, 1995). Webquests aim to provide the kind of information learners need to carry out a search alongside a reflective framework for making sure they get the most out of the experience and process information deeply. A typical webquest has the following elements:

- an introduction to the topic and the aim of tasks;

- the task, which is typically enquiry or problem-based this may include a breakdown of stages and roles for group members;

- resources, a list of websites or search tools recommended for the task;

- Reflection on the task, perhaps including a summary of what has been learned and an evaluation of its usefulness.

A webquest generator can be found at: www.aula21.net/Wqfacil/webeng.htm. However, it is straightforward to construct a web page yourself that includes the necessary elements. If your school or college has a virtual learning environment this will have a web page builder function.

Using a virtual learning environment

The technical bit

Ofsted (2009) have defined a virtual learning environment (or VLE) as 'a computer-based system that helps learning' (p. 8). This is a deliberately broad term used to avoid bias between the different ways of and tools for organising learning materials online. In a managerial sense, then, any website on which learning materials are organised can be called a virtual learning environment.

Taking learning online

More technically speaking, a VLE is a particular sort of website or content management system adapted to education in the following ways:

- A VLE is structured in such a way that material is organised into courses, and within courses into logical divisions like topics or weeks.

- Students can register on a VLE and access their course or courses.

- A VLE has education-specific tools, for example for building quizzes, submitting assignments and recording marks.

- A VLE has various levels of access to that teachers can create courses and materials while students can just see resources and complete tasks.

There are a number of VLE systems around. Some, like Blackboard, WebCT and Frog, are commercial. Others, like Moodle, are free and open-source. Several studies (e.g. Suri and Schuhmacher, 2008) have concluded that pedagogically Moodle is the best system, although other factors such as ease of linking up to the school or college Management Information System also play a part in your institutional choice of system.

Table 5.3 Key app: Moodle

Publisher	Moodle.org	http://moodle.org/	Licence: Free & open-source	
Platform	Windows YES	Mac YES	Linux YES	Online YES
Also consider	At the time of writing, I wouldn't. Other options tend to be expensive and less well featured			
Mobile position	Moodle apps exist for iOS and Android. Most features also work in a mobile browser			

The theory bit

According to Dillenbourg (2000), a VLE is not simply an educational website but a *designed* learning space, put together to enable a set of functions. Caruso and Kvavik (2005) identify organising course information, communication with learners, posting of course resources and assessment tools. Management of learner information such as results of assessments can be done using a VLE; however, it is increasingly the norm to use a purpose-built Management Information System for this. As Caruso and Kvavik say, VLE technology undoubtedly has the potential to enhance learning. Think back to the 2008 JISC report mentioned in Chapter 1 (see p. 5); a well-designed and used VLE may help reduce costs and increase retention and achievement through making sure learners can always access materials even when they are not in class for whatever reason. It can make learning more inclusive by giving access to a whole course to those who would be unable to attend in person.

The tricky aspect of VLE use is to make it conform to principles of effective learning. Although a learner has to undertake some activity simply to access a VLE, getting them to be *really* active, making choices and engaging intellectually with tasks, takes a lot more thought. The way most teachers use VLE technology tends to position the learner as a relatively passive consumer of information; this is in marked contrast to the relationship between user and app in most contexts outside formal education (Selwyn, 2007). If a course is dominated by static teacher-generated resources then we inevitably limit learners' self-regulation and personal agency (Turker and Zingel, 2008). Increasingly, VLEs (notably Moodle) have been designed with this in mind, and do include tools to create online forums, wikis and chat rooms. However, to use Moodle to its potential we need to use these functions.

The practice

Installing your own VLE

If your school or college does not have a VLE or you dislike it it's actually surprisingly straightforward to set up your own, although it's worth checking whether your management will see this move as innovation or subversion! Many web-hosting companies include an auto-installer, which can install Moodle on your website for you. You don't need any other website infrastructure if you don't want, just your Moodle, and this is installed more or less at the touch of a button. See http://moodle.org for instructions on setting up courses and registering students in Moodle.

Structuring a course on a VLE

This could easily be a whole book in itself, so this is a really brief account. A VLE can be used in different ways. If your PTBs give you a choice, I strongly suggest that you structure courses by topic rather than week. Weekly layouts can appeal to managers because they make you look well-organised and elaborately planned. However, you only have to have one unplanned absence or a trip arranged after the VLE is constructed to throw your weekly plan out and confuse students about where they should be for weeks to follow. Topic-formats are much more flexible. Under each topic you have the opportunity to add static resources such as documents, presentations and links, and more interactive ones such as quizzes, assessments and, depending on the system, forums, chat-rooms, wikis, etc.

Integrate social media

To make a course page look and feel more like the sort of online tools learners would use outside formal education, consider embedding some social media. If you are using Moodle there is the functionality to add RSS feeds, and if you can generate a Twitter widget from a site you'd like your learners to follow (the easiest way to do this is at: http://twitterforweb.com) you can paste the embed code into an HTML block. See Figure 5.7 for an example of a Twitter feed.

Creating learning hubs

The default layout of Moodle lists resources one under the other. This 'flat' architecture is deliberate and designed to avoid the multiple layers of folders that characterise other VLEs. An example of a topic is shown in Figure 5.6.

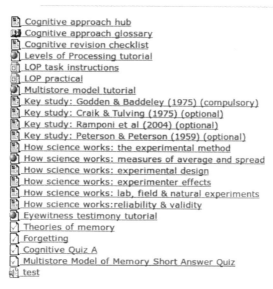

Figure 5.6 The default listing of resources in Moodle. Also known as the 'scroll of death!'

Taking learning online

However, once your course is mature you will probably have quite a lot of resources there, and a massive list looks unattractive and requires the 'scroll of death' – something learners tend not to have to do much of in other modern websites. An alternative is to create a webpage for each topic and link to major resources from here. Resources can be connected by a narrative outlining the topic and its assessment. Resources and activities should be sequenced logically; for example, beginning with an introductory video or fascinator exercise and following up with a handout and/or presentation, then showing the kind of assessment learners need to prepare for. This sort of web page is called a learning hub. An example is shown in Figure 5.7.

Adding a web page is as simple as turning on editing and clicking the 'add activity or resource' button and selecting 'page'. This is shown in Figure 5.8. This menu will look slightly different if you are using a different version of Moodle but the content should be much the same.

Figure 5.7 An example of a learning hub

Figure 5.8 Adding a web page in Moodle 2.4

Add some eye candy

This is in one sense frivolity, but anything that makes a learning hub or course front page look more congruent with other online tools is likely to help with learner engagement. One example of this is to embed a flash 'e-book' or 'e-magazine' into a hub. There are numerous sites – like Zamzar (www.zamzar.com) that will convert a PowerPoint presentation into a Shockwave Flash file that can be embedded in any web page. Don't be put off by terms like 'book' or 'magazine'. Anything that can be made into a PowerPoint or PDF can be converted to a SWF. You might, for example, want to display a past exam paper or a multipage assignment inside a web page.

Post a limited number of static resources and use the interactive features

Your course will lose its visual impact if it is too crowded. It will also get hard for learners to locate what they are looking for. You don't necessarily have to have every handout and every presentation available online. If you are determined to do this, try packaging resources into a few large ones – a booklet containing all your handouts for a topic, for example. Interactive tools include the following:

- forum
- wiki
- instant messaging
- chat room
- quizzes.

Figure 5.9 The menu used to insert interactive features in Moodle

Of course there is a steep investment of time required to populate a course with all these resources, but once it's done properly that's the basics of your preparation done until the next curriculum revision, leaving you free to be more creative with fine-tuning your personalisation, etc.

Creating online questions

There are a range of existing quizzes to be found on the Net. You can also download good (and free) software called Hot Potatoes to make your own quizzes. Your VLE will probably have some tools for quiz creation but these are permanently part of your VLE – it is not straightforward to extract your quizzes and take them with you when you move jobs. Nowadays tools like Hot Potatoes integrate into a VLE so that test scores are automatically recorded and can generate separate files that you can keep for future use. Hot Potatoes generates a range of quiz types including crosswords, multiple choice, cloze and matching.

Hot Potatoes is not available for mobile devices, and the quiz generators that are available don't have anywhere near the same kind of functionality. For iPads, consider Quiz Maker (commercial but not too expensive), or Quiz Creator (free with adverts, cheap without) for Android.

Table 5.4 Key app: Hot Potatoes

Publisher	Half-Baked Software	http://hotpot. uvic.ca/	Licence: Free but not open-source
Platform	Windows YES	Mac YES	Linux YES
Also consider	Quizfaber		
Mobile position	Not available for iOS or Android		

Figure 5.10 The Hot Potatoes interface

Encouraging learners to use the VLE

A lot of us in the past have fallen into what e-learning folk call the 'build it and they will come' trap! We can build the most sophisticated and useful VLE course in the world, and yet most teachers' experience is that many learners will not spontaneously engage with it. It is important to have a strategy to get learners in the habit of working from a VLE.

- Use it from the start of your course. Once learners are in the habit of working in a particular way it is hard to persuade them to try something new. A compulsory activity at the beginning of your course is often a good plan.

- Make sure it works, and that learners know how to use it. Many learners will give unfamiliar technology one go but no more! That one attempt has to be a successful experience. If you can get hold of an IT suite, have a class session to iron out any individual difficulties. I would also screencast (see p. 83) how to use the course and make sure every learner has easy access to the video.

- Put something worth doing on there. Once learners are convinced there is a real benefit to them there is a good chance they will overcome any technophobia and technical difficulties and make the effort to master the VLE.

Delivering lessons online

The technical bit

VLEs are designed to organise learning at the whole-course level. There are times though when what you really want is to deliver a lesson or topic online. There are various online platforms with which you can do this but I particularly like Blendspace. Blendspace allows you to mash documents, presentations, videos, etc., into a page, and add audio or written instructions and quizzes. An example of a Blendspace lesson is shown in Figure 5.11.

Table 5.5 Key app: Blendspace

Publisher	Blendspace	www.blendspace. com	Licence: Free for teachers, paid for whole schools with extra functionality	
Platform	Windows YES	Mac YES	Linux YES	Online YES
Also consider	Nearpod			
Mobile position	Dedicated apps not currently available but works well in a mobile browser			

Popular culture

Figure 5.11 A Blendspace lesson

Theory and practice

Blendspace is not designed to replace a VLE, although in principle there is no particular reason why you couldn't upload a whole course to it. What Blendspace does extremely well is allow you to post a complete lesson or topic online. If you are planning to teach a lesson or topic remotely, for example to distance learners or on a snow day, simply post instructions followed by whatever documents, presentations and videos you need, and, if you wish, check understanding with a quiz.

Online back-up tools and e-portfolios

I have seen some tragedies such as failed A-levels and many more minor but irritating cock-ups happen – and others waiting to happen – because teachers and learners don't necessarily back up their work. Learners should always back up coursework and in fact any project work online. Even the humble group project can be easily derailed because the one learner with the project files is off sick. All this can be avoided by proper use of back-up tools. However, we can also take online storage to the next level and help learners keep an e-portfolio.

The technical bit

Online back-up tools

Online storage and back-up are big business, and there is a range of apps that will give you a good chunk of free storage space – in the hope that you will eventually need to buy more! All the following apps will integrate in some way to your desktop so you can save or back-up online directly without going to the website. See Table 5.6, but be aware that some features may change over the lifespan of this book.

Some of these criteria need a little teasing out. If a file syncs (synchronises) this means that as you update it the online version (and, if applicable, the versions on your other computers) updates as well. Syncing may be instant – when you hit 'save' – or scheduled, i.e. all files are backed up at a time of your choosing. For learners it is important to be able to access old versions of a document – this allows those engaged in project work to experiment then abandon failed directions and, perhaps more critically, it means that a malicious individual cannot delete all copies of a learner's coursework. Being able to easily create a

Table 5.6 Comparison of online back-up solutions

App	Web address	Free storage	Instant sync	Scheduled sync	Access prior document versions	Share folders
DropBox	www.dropbox.com	2 GB	YES	NO	YES	YES
Minus	http://minus.com/	1o GB	NO	NO	NO	YES
Spideroak	https://spideroak.com/	2 GB	NO	YES	YES	YES
Box	https://www.box.com/	5 GB	YES	NO	YES	YES (not Linux)

shared folder means a group can work on a project without one member exposing all the back-ups to public scrutiny.

Mahara: An e-portfolio app

E-portfolios began life as online storage for learners, but the concept has rapidly evolved so that modern e-portfolios include a range of other functions. Mahara, the New Zealand government's e-portfolio solution, is currently emerging as the 'industry standard' tool. Mahara is free and open-source but as it runs on a server rather than a desktop you will need a website to host it. If you are running Mahara independently of your school or college you will need to pay for hosting. The Mahara 'splash screen' is shown in Figure 5.12.

As you can see from figure 5.12, you can upload files for storage (no sync function at the time of writing), but learners can also keep a diary, put together a CV, create web pages, discuss on a forum, share pages and network through 'friends' (in the Facebook sense) and groups. Users create a personal profile in order to create a sense of ownership and congruence with other online apps.

Figure 5.12 The Mahara splash screen

Table 5.7 Key app: Mahara

Publisher	Mahara	https://mahara. org/	Licence: Free and open-source	
Platform	Windows YES	Mac YES	Linux YES	Online YES
Also consider	ClassDroid			
Mobile position	Mahara apps are available for iOS and Android			

The theory and practice

There is no educational theory underlying the idea of backing up data – it's common sense! However, the ability to share documents and folders really makes a difference to collaboration, so these tools do support the principle of interactivity in learning. E-portfolios are more interesting. They represent an attempt to bring together several aspects of learning – they facilitate collaboration and interaction, whilst the journal function supports reflectivity and the CV career planning. Functionally, you can replicate most of these tools on Box, however Mahara is an extremely attractive and user-friendly environment.

At the time of writing e-portfolios are very new technology and it is unclear which features and functions will really capture learners' imagination. It may be that different schools and colleges run with different ideas, so that one will focus on using the journal to encourage reflective learning while another focuses on CV writing. A knee-jerk institutional response to the existence of e-portfolios is probably quite a bad idea – once they are introduced badly to your school or college your learners (not to mention colleagues!) will require a lot of convincing to give them a second try. As an institution it is well worth stepping back and considering the potential of e-portfolios and what needs you see them satisfying, and only then devising a strategy for their introduction.

Going interactive with Web 2.0

If you dabble in ICT you will probably have heard about Web 2.0, but let's try to pin the idea down a bit more precisely. The term 'Web 2.0' has been around since around 2004–5. According to McLoughlin and Lee (2007) Web 2.0 is 'a second generation, or more personalised, communicative form of the World Wide Web that emphasises active participation, connectivity, collaboration and sharing of knowledge and ideas among users' (p. 665). Some commentators see Web 2.0 as a distinct second wave of the Internet, representing a paradigm shift from how the Net was originally used. However, others (notably Tim Berners-Lee – the original developer of the Internet) see it as a set of natural developments in what the Internet was always intended to be.

The technical bit

A number of quite different applications fall under the umbrella of Web 2.0. Here are some of the major ones:

- *Wiki*: a user-controlled website where learners can write the content and comment on each other's contributions.

- *Blog*: a website in which content appears in the order it is posted, most recent first, and on which other users can comment. Tumblr deserves a special mention here because it is a multimedia blog, designed to make it easy to post audio and video material as well as verbal information.

- *Social network*: an online community of individuals who can view some of each other's web space and communicate with one another.

- *Forum*: an online discussion environment.

- *Chat room*: a synchronous (real-time) online discussion environment where discussions can take place between any number of users much as they would face to face.

- *RSS* (really simple syndication): A feed for channelling information from one website to another so that when one site is updated so is the other.

Table 5.8 Examples of Web 2.0 tools

Blogging tools	Twitter	https://twitter.com
	WordPress	http://wordpress.com
	Blogger	www.blogger.com/start
Multimedia blogging	Tumblr	www.tumblr.com
Wiki builder	WikiSpaces	www.wikispaces.com
	Wikia	www.wikia.com/Wikia
Private social network builder	Spruz	www.spruz.com
	Ning	http://uk.ning.com
	Edmodo	www.edmodo.com
Forums	MakeForum	www.makeforum.org
	Lefora	www.lefora.com
Social bookmarking	Digg	http://digg.com
	Delicious	http://delicious.com
	Stumbleupon	www.stumbleupon.com

The theory bit

We are currently teaching the first few cohorts of what e-learning theorists call 'digital natives', young people who have never known a time without ICT, and they are thoroughly used to Web 2.0, which is characterised by high levels of control and interactivity (O'Reilly, 2005). The problem with VLE technology is that it affords a top-down process with teachers providing static resources for students to passively download and use. *But this is not how young people use the Internet.* Outside education, students spend time social-networking, blogging, contributing to as well as taking from wikis, subscribing to RSS feeds, file-sharing and social-bookmarking. All these types of app position the user as a prosumer rather than consumer of information (Auinger, 2009).

Web 2.0 ways of using the Internet are highly active and interactive processes in which students make and act on decisions rather than being passively led. Web 2.0 tools have not necessarily been designed with education in mind, and don't particularly lend themselves to the sort of tightly controlled learning teachers working to an examined course tend to favour. The trade-off, however, is that Web 2.0 apps have a good cultural fit with the customs of digital natives and they therefore facilitate very good levels of engagement. To put it another way, where VLE tech is great for formal education if you can just get learners to use it, Web 2.0 tech is great for engaging learners but needs a lot of thinking about if it is going to help learners negotiate narrow, content-heavy specifications.

The practice

Run a VLE and supplement it with Web 2.0

While some e-learning experts see VLEs and Web 2.0 as rival technology and fiercely take the side of one or other, there is no reason why they should not be used together. The choice becomes between using the functionality of the VLE and linking to specialist external sites. Some VLEs, notably Moodle, have some Web 2.0 functionality, and are quite capable of running blogs, wikis, etc. However, there are also numerous free online resources purpose-made for Web 2.0 development. There is a trade-off between the benefits and costs of each of these approaches. External sites are typically more attractive than VLE Web 2.0 functions and have a better cultural fit with the sites your learners use outside education. On the other hand, apps internal to the VLE are under your control and quicker to operate.

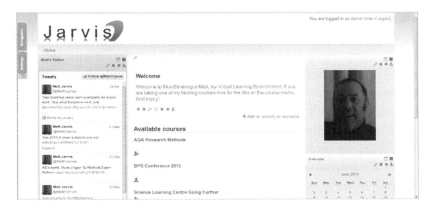

Figure 5.13 This Moodle site has an embedded Twitter feed (ignore the ugly git in the picture)

There is no doubt that learners use Web 2.0 for informal learning (Selwyn, 2007). However, this is not the same as saying that Web 2.0 necessarily lends itself to classroom use, and you can be forgiven for wondering just what to do with a wiki or forum, particularly if you don't use these things yourself. The following are just some simple suggestions.

- *Use a social network to create a group identity for your classes or courses*: One way to boost enthusiasm for a course or a sense of collective identity in a group is to put them on a social network. There are (very sensibly!) strict child protection guidelines that restrict the interaction of learners and teachers via public social networks like Facebook. However, it is possible to set up a private social network using an app like Ning or Spruz.

Figure 5.13 A Ning network

Very similar results can be obtained using an education-specific tool like Edmodo or an e-portfolio builder like Mahara. The question is not so much around functionality as learner engagement. This may require a bit of trial and error as you check out which approach grabs your learners.

- *Application of subject matter to real-life*: This can be done using blog or forum technology. Cut and paste a news story or link to it and ask learners to explain, collectively, in groups or individually, how their subject could be applied to the event. The event could be anything from unusual weather (geography) to a medical breakthrough (biology). The critical rule is that each group or individual must add something to the discussion. The advantage of having this on a forum or blog over conventional paper methods is that learners can learn from each others' ideas and internalise the skills of application.

- *Peer marking*: One way to teach students how to use awarding body mark-schemes is to place examples on a blog or wiki and have learners peer-mark them, then argue for their choice of mark. The advantage of doing this in a Web 2.0 environment is the ability to follow each others' logic and actively construct one's own view.

- *Peer work enhancement*: This can be done using a blog or wiki. Provide an exam question and a basic answer. Ask learners to each produce an expanded version. The rule here is that they can look at each others' ideas but their wording must be their own. This allows learners to develop their exam skills, making use of the exam-savvies of their peers.

- *Class-generated notes*: This one probably works best with wiki technology, and it requires that you either have strong nerves or are prepared to intervene, because it involves learners taking on considerable responsibility. Give a class a small section of the curriculum and have them put together their own resources. You'll need to cue them in with the appropriate content and some likely sources of information.

- *Pooled revision resources*: Learners revise in different ways, and there is never enough time for them to try all strategies. One way around this is to have students pool their flash cards, mind-maps, concept maps, podcasts and vodcasts via a Web 2.0 environment. Private social networks probably work best for this.

'Mashing up' online apps

We have already established that both VLE and Web 2.0 technology have their strengths and weaknesses. One way to reconcile these is to 'mash' all your online tools into a single web page, sometimes called a MUPPLE (mashed-up personal learning environment).

The technical bit

Probably the simplest way to mash up your online resources is online using a site called NetVibes. Create an account and add a new page. You'll be presented with a set of (annoying) demonstration pages. Delete these and use the 'add content' button (top left) to insert the sites you wish to have mashed in.

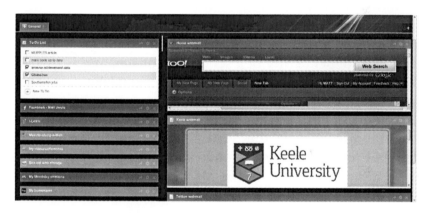

Figure 5.15 An example of a MUPPLE

Table 5.9 Key app: NetVibes

Publisher	NetVibes	www.netibes.com	Licence: Free but not open-source
Platform	Online ONLY		
Also consider	iGoogle		
Mobile position	Apps are available for iOS and Android, but Netvibes is at its best on a large screen		

Content is added to your page via widgets. The most important widget is 'webpage'. This allows you to add any existing page to yours. You will probably want to add a number of pages. There are specific widgets for sites like Facebook, and a range of others with educational applications such as 'to-do list' and a range of search tools. Select a theme and layout, and you're away!

The theory bit

Taraghi, Ebner and Schaffert (2009) define MUPPLEs as 'learning applications where the learner can integrate and organise distributed online information, resources and contacts, as well as to provide content' (p. 16). According to Auinger (2009) a key feature of a MUPPLE is that it is hosted independently of a school or college, and is owned by and under the control of the individual learner. This personal ownership is important in creating a sense of agency in the learner, and is in direct contrast to the top-down model of the Virtual Learning Environment. Studies (e.g. Jarvis, 2011b) have shown that learners show a significant preference for MUPPLEs over a traditional VLE interface, rating MUPPLEs as more attractive, user-friendly, congruent with ICT use outside formal education and more useful.

The practice

There is a paradox here in that although we as educators have a pretty good idea of what pages and apps we think should be mashed into a MUPPLE, a crucial element of the MUPPLE concept is user control. Teachers will need to gently guide learners through the process of constructing their MUPPLEs; however, we must also take a step back and (possibly through gritted teeth!) let learners incorporate sites of their own choosing. I would always recommend rather than prescribe sites and widgets to mash up, but here are some suggestions:

- your course VLE

- personal and school/college e-mail

- personal social network, e.g. Facebook

- course social network, e.g. Ning

- to-do list

- subject dictionary and/or search engine

- social bookmarking app, e.g. Digg

- online back-up/e-portfolio.

There is overlap in the functionality of some of these apps, so for example you probably won't need an e-portfolio and a course social network. You may want to mash in a wiki or blog site, or alternatively you might want to use these functions in your course VLE.

Conclusions and reflections

Some of the best tools in educational technology run online, and being online has the potential to introduce whole new dimensions in activity and interactivity to teaching. There is every reason to be excited about the potential offered by the Internet itself and in particular by VLE and Web 2.0 apps. Working online is probably the aspect of e-learning that offers you the greatest opportunities to stretch yourself and incorporate cutting edge techniques into your pedagogy. Some of the ideas described in this chapter are a little more advanced technologically than those outlined elsewhere in this book. However, some techniques are straightforward, and you don't need to be anywhere near a fully-fledged web designer to do everything in this chapter. The main thing to remember – and I'm unashamedly labouring this point – is to think in terms of effective learning, and to bring in technology where you see an opportunity to achieve this.

CHAPTER 6

Personalising the learner experience with technology

By the end of this chapter you should be able to:

- appreciate the diversity of learner needs and the potential for personalising their experience using technology;
- know how to use settings and accessibility tools to make common apps more user-friendly to a range of learners;
- understand a range of user-friendly file formats, including Braille and DAISY, and use appropriate tools to create and manage them;
- be familiar with e-book formats and produce e-books for learners;
- use visualisation tools, including mind maps, concept maps and flow charts, to help learners organise ideas.

In education, catering for the needs of a diverse range of learners is not a luxury but absolutely central to what we do. To put it bluntly, no one pays us to be of use to some of our learners. In practice we won't always get this sort of personalisation right – there are simply too many variables to take into account, too little information available and too little time to plan how to make best use of the information we have. That said, we should always try in good faith to personalise our learners' experiences and consider what strategies will help us meet individual needs. There are a number of ways in which technology can help with this. In particular, technology allows us to present and organise information in different formats, so that learners with difficulties in dealing with information in one form can access it in another. In this chapter I focus on the following ideas:

- accessibility tools and tips to make common software such as word processors and browsers more user-friendly for learners with visual difficulties or dyslexia;

- converting resources to formats like Braille and DAISY that are designed to be accessible to learners with visual difficulties;

- converting resources to e-book formats that allow learners to easily access them using tablets and e-readers;

- tools to help learners with auditory difficulties make the most of speech in the classroom and using multimedia;

- tools to help learners organise and visualise verbal material.

By the time they get to you some of your learners will have had assessments and diagnoses, and they may receive specialist help, possibly including specialist hardware and software. This chapter may not be of particular help to you in meeting the needs of those students – they are likely to have access to expensive high-quality tools. However, the chances are that you also have contact with some learners who have either never been assessed or who do not meet thresholds for specialist help and resources but who can benefit from a bit of personalised techy help.

This chapter may be helpful for these learners because I can make suggestions for tools and ways of working that are free or cheap and are straightforward to implement.

There is quite a small overlap between professionals who specialise in e-learning and those with a good knowledge of diverse educational needs. This means that these tools and techniques discussed here are not common knowledge amongst teachers. However, they probably should be – introducing them to the right learner at the right moment may change their whole experience of education for the better.

Making common software more accessible

Browser settings and add-ons

The technical bit

All the common browsers have settings that can be adjusted to change the appearance of websites. You should, for example, be able to zoom in, enlarge text or remove page styling so that text alone is displayed. For example, in Firefox see in Figure 6.1a and b what happens when you select *Page style* then *no style* in the *View* menu.

However, you can gain rather more control over the appearance of web pages using accessibility add-ons. There are a number of these in existence, most being aimed at particular browsers. However, one piece of kit exists that stands out as comprehensive, remarkably easy to use and compatible with all major browsers. This is the AT Bar, shown in Figure 6.2.

To install the AT Bar go to www.atbar.org/atbar-lite and follow the instructions – it's as simple as dragging a button to your bookmarks then clicking on it there to activate. With the AT Bar you can do the following to a webpage:

- increase and decrease text size;
- change font;
- spell check;

Personalising with technology

Figure 6.1a The Routledge homepage in normal view

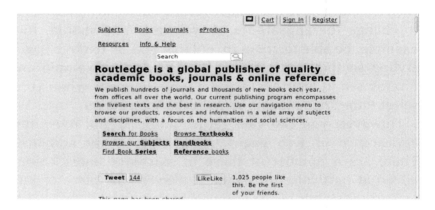

Figure 6.1b The same website with no style

Figure 6.2 The AT Bar

- link to dictionary – just highlight a word and click for a definition;

- read text aloud;

- view in readability mode, which leaves images but removes background colour and formats text in a generally readable size and font;

- change page styles, either manually or by selecting a pre-set style of appearance often found to be user-friendly to learners with dyslexia or visual impairment.

Table 6.1 Key app: AT Bar

Publisher	ATBar.org	http://www. atbar.org	Licence: Free
Platform	Windows YES	Mac YES	Linux YES
Also consider	Web Accessibility Toolbar (Windows & Internet Explorer), Juicy Studio Accessibility Toolbar (Firefox)		
Mobile position	Not suitable for iOS or Android		

Tools like the AT Bar are helpful for static content on websites, but video material presents more of a problem. Both Hearing and visually impaired learners can struggle with video. An accessibility app you might find useful here is YouTube's Captions. This provides subtitles to YouTube videos. At the time of writing this is at an early stage of development, but hearing-impaired learners may find it of some use.

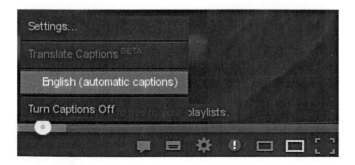

Figure 6.3 YouTube's Captions feature

Mobile platforms approach this kind of accessibility differently. If you work with an iPad or Android tablet then your operating system has the inbuilt ability to zoom in, increase text size and convert text to speech. Apps also exist that allow you to work in Braille and learn sign language, and for learners with speech problems there are apps that will speak pre-configured phrases. In addition there are multiple apps available on iTunes (the Apple store) and Google Play (the Android app store) to help meet the needs of individual users.

The theory bit

Changing the appearance of a website may make it easier for learners to work with it for a number of reasons. Eliminating animations, tables and background colour (as achieved by the AT Bar readability mode) can all reduce cognitive load. This can benefit anyone but may particularly useful to learners who struggle with concentration or who have short-term memory problems.

Another important factor in the accessibility of a web page is its contrast ratio. This is the difference (in colour and brightness) between the text colour and its background. The World Wide Web Consortium publish guidelines on contrast ratios (see www.w3.org/TR/WCAG for more details) but these are very technical! To put it simply, there is a scale from 1:1 (no contrast) to 21:1 (maximum contrast, black on white or vice versa). For visually impaired learners the higher the contrast ratio the easier text is to read on a screen. The larger the text the less contrast ratio is required.

If you want to assess your school or college website/VLE you can do so free using this site: http://www.accesskeys. org/tools/color-contrast.html. There are two levels of response to a failing site. First – and strictly under the terms of the Disability Discrimination Act you should do this – you can adjust the colours on your site. The second response, which is not mutually exclusive with the first, is to educate your learners about tools like the AT Bar that make it very easy to adjust contrast ratio to what is comfortable to the individual. The advantage of this approach is that learners will be empowered to make best use of the whole Web.

Figure 6.4 High and low contrast ratios

Most of the emphasis in published guidelines has been on making contrast higher than many web designers would like for the sake of users with visual impairments. For teachers the situation is made more complex by the fact that learners with dyslexia often find very high contrast ratios uncomfortable. I find a ratio of around 16:1 is generally okay for most learners.

The practice

Although most or all of your learners will have used the Internet, don't fall into the trap of thinking that this experience means they have a sophisticated understanding of how to use it effectively. There is little awareness in the general public about accessibility tools so I recommend instructing all learners in the use of the AT Bar. Most won't use it but it will *really* help a minority.

Bear in mind though that when we are dealing with individual learners who have a mild or undiagnosed difficulty they will have developed coping mechanisms. Depending on the individual these coping mechanisms may include denial of the problem and resistance to help.

These learners will benefit from sensitive individual work. It may be worth whoever is the most appropriate person in the organisation sitting down with an individual and together trying all the settings on the AT Bar in some real learning tasks and exploring how much use each is.

Always remember as well that even individuals with the same diagnosis will vary massively, not only in their history and coping strategies but also cognitively. One person's dyslexia is not necessarily the same as another's, so try not to make assumptions about what will benefit whom. This kind of work is always a collaborative journey, with you and the learner discovering together what works for them. The technology simply gives you avenues to explore.

Office software

Different as word processors and presenters appear at face value, some of the same tips and tools will benefit both so I am going to consider them together here.

The technology bit

Word processors and presenters allow you considerable control over the visual appearance of documents and presentations, so you can achieve a lot without specialist tools. You can, for example, vary background and text colour, hence contrast ratio is very much under your control – particularly in a presentation. If you have no access to colour photocopying and are concerned about black text on white paper you can use coloured paper or issue learners coloured transparencies to place over text resources. You can also vary font and font size, line spacing, column width, etc. These are all accessibility features of the software.

There are also some other apps you might want to consider to improve accessibility. You may, for example, wish to have something read documents aloud. This can be done in various ways. There are different apps available for different operating systems and office suites. Apps also vary considerably by price. Looking at what is free, you might want to consider those listed in Table 6.2.

Table 6.2 Key apps: text to speech tools for office software

Tool	Platform	Office suite	Found at	Licence
Browsealoud	Windows	MS Office	http://www. browsealoud.co.uk	Free
i-Work text to speech	Mac	i-Work	http://www.apple. com/accessibility/ macosx/ literacylearning. html	Commercial
Read Text Extension	Linux	Libre-Office	http://extensions. libreoffice.org/ extension-center/ read-text	Free & open-source
ETTS	Android	Stand-alone	https://play.google. com/store/apps/ details?id=com easysolutions. easytexttospeechfree &hl=en_GB	Free version
Natural Reader	iOS	Stand-alone	https://itunes.apple. com/us/app/ naturalreader-text-to-speech/ id598798210?mt=8	Free

A really simple alternative if you want to hear a piece of text read out is to paste the text into Google Translate. Just go to http://translate.google.com and paste your text in to the left pane. It will show up as English in the right pane and you just click the speaker icon at the bottom of the right pane. It will be read out in a remarkably clear and natural-sounding voice.

Text-to-speech tools are well established. For some learners, however, a good speech-to-text application is critical.

Personalising with technology

The industry standard tool for Windows and Mac is Dragon Naturally Speaking. This is not cheap at around £80 for a single user licence, but as it works extremely well and there is no comparable free alternative at the time of writing you may decide it is worth the money. For something a little simpler, but free and adequate for many people, try Speech Recogniser. This is a Google Chrome application. Although Speech Recogniser runs in the Chrome browser it works offline. You will find Speech Recogniser in the Chrome Web Store.

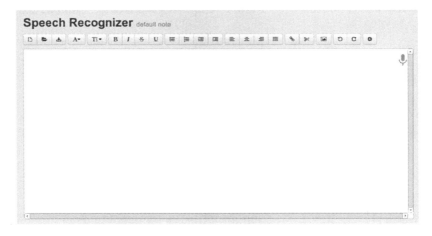

Figure 6.5 The Speech Recogniser interface

Speech recogniser is extremely easy to use. Just plug in a microphone and speak and text will appear in the box. It won't have punctuation or capitals but you can cut and paste the text into a word processor and edit it there.

Speech to text is an area where mobile platforms really come into their own, there being a good range of free good-quality apps around. For Android try Listnote Speech/ Text Notepad (free version available), or for iOS consider OpenEars.

The theory and practice

The same principles that guide web accessibility can be applied to using office software. Slides and documents are generally easier to read if text is larger, lines are well spaced, columns are narrower, margins are wider and contrast ratios are optimal. For anyone for whom reading text is harder than for the typical person – this could be the result of dyslexia, visual impairment, concentration or short-term memory problems – this is likely to be particularly important. You can make slides and documents more accessible by narrowing text columns, increasing font size, increasing line spacing, narrowing columns, increasing margins and setting your contrast ratio high enough to be clear but not so high as to be uncomfortable to those with dyslexia.

Text-to-speech and speech-to-text tools may also be helpful to some learners. For anyone for whom reading is a problem, a text-to-speech tool allows comprehension of words without visual processing. Another group of learners may have more problems with writing, perhaps

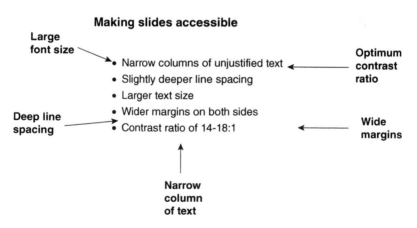

Figure 6.6 A standard bullet point slide with basic accessibility features

through dyslexia or perhaps because of a physical disability affecting hand co-ordination. For this group a speech-to text tool like Dragon or Speech Recogniser may be helpful.

All the provisos discussed on p. 135 apply here. Although text-to-speech and speech-to-text tools are extremely helpful for some learners, the pedagogical skills of working with individuals to explore what will help them are paramount. This is really why teachers rather than any other group of professionals are the best placed to work with tools like this, even though this may mean a steep learning curve if you aren't currently particularly tech-savvy.

Working with user-friendly file formats

Standard file formats are great in the sense that most teachers and learners will at least some of the time be able to access some hardware and software that can display them. They may, however, not be the most user-friendly formats for learners with particular learning needs. My aim in this section is to introduce you to Braille and DAISY, two formats that may be particularly helpful for learners with visual impairments.

The technical bit

Braille is a 3D reading and writing system that involves representing letters by bumps, technically called *divots*. Braille can be printed with an embossing printer or read from a refreshable Braille display. All you need to make resources available to learners in Braille format is to be able to translate text into Braille. Fortunately this is much more straightforward than you might think. There are a number of websites where you can upload files or cut and paste text, then simply click to translate. I like Braille Translator: http://www.brailletranslator.org.

Figure 6.7 Braille can be easily produced at brailletranslator.org

If you prefer a downloadable Braille translator there are numerous commercial programmes around but these can be extremely expensive and tend to be for Windows only. For a free and open-source alternative try NAT Braille. This works on Windows, Mac and Linux systems, and can be found at http://sourceforge.net/projects/nat-braille. There are good free tools available for Android (e.g. Braille Writer) mobile platforms, and since iOS 7 Braille translation is inbuilt.

Another system favoured by many people with visual impairments is DAISY. DAISY is an international standard for talking books. Don't be put off by the word 'books' however. You can save any document as a DAISY file. To do this you need to install an add-in to Microsoft Word (http://sourceforge.net/projects/openxml-daisy) or LibreOffice Writer (http://odt2daisy.sourceforge.net/about). This will allow you to save as DAISY. One tip, though; one of the reasons DAISY files are so user-friendly is that they can be navigated. To allow this your document must have properly formatted headings. Just using 'bold', etc., to format your headings won't work with DAISY; you need to actually select the appropriate level for each heading from the styles menu. You then need a DAISY reader in order to read the files. Examples are shown in the Key Apps box.

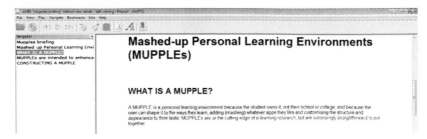

Figure 6.8 A DAISY document being displayed in AMIS, a free
DAISY reader for Windows. Note the navigation pane
on the left

Readers like AMIS make a document extremely easy
to follow. The document is read out aloud (you can select
an appropriate speed), and at the same time you can follow the text as it is read by watching the highlighter move
through the document. All your headings are shown in the
navigation pane, so you can jump straight to wherever
you want in a document.

Table 6.3 Key apps: DAISY readers

Tool	Platform	Found at	Licence
AMIS	Windows	http://www.daisy.org/amis/download	Free & open-source
Olearia	Mac	http://code.google.com/p/olearia/	Free & open-source
DAISY Book Reader	Linux	http://sourceforge.net/projects/openxml-daisy/	Free & open-source
Darwin Reader	Android	https://play.google.com/store/apps/details?id=com.ndu.mobile.daisy.full	Commercial
Daisy Worm	iOS	https://itunes.apple.com/us/app/daisyworm/id383777731?mt=8&ign-msr=http%3A%2F%2Fwww.daisy.org%2Ftools%2F1463	Commercial

The theory and practice

Where Braille is meant primarily for people with severely impaired vision, DAISY will be of more help to those with mild to moderate visual impairment. Many learners with dyslexia – and any other cognitive problem affecting reading – will also find that DAISY makes long text-heavy documents much less intimidating. In fact I recommend trying DAISY to anyone!

You may go through your whole teaching career without encountering a Braille user, and if you do so it may be that they and their carers are familiar with the appropriate technology. On the other hand you may work with a learner who has recently lost their sight. In this scenario it will be very much a question of working together to explore what works for the individual. DAISY is a different kettle of fish. All teachers work with learners that, by virtue of mild visual impairment, dyslexia, short-term memory or attention problems find it hard to engage with extended text. For a substantial number of these DAISY can make a real difference, and I really recommend that all teachers get familiar with it.

You can easily make resources available in DAISY and Braille formats on a virtual learning environment, but beware of the 'build it and they will come' trap! It will be well worth demonstrating DAISY in particular, and using an IT suite to give learners hands-on experience (don't forget the headphones!). You may also find it really helpful to introduce DAISY to learners in one-to-one tutorials.

Going mobile with e-book formats

You'll certainly have heard of e-books as a rapidly growing business. What you may not realise, though, is just how straightforward it is to create e-books from your exist-ing resources. At the time of writing we are undergoing a cultural change where the use of e-books is growing so rapidly that, although the image of learners reading your handouts and worksheets on a Kindle or Kobo may seem far-fetched, actually it may become the norm within the lifetime of this book.

The technical bit

Although e-books can be read on a conventional com-puter they really come into their own when used with an e-reader. Common e-readers include the Kindle, Nook and Kobo. E-books come in a range of file formats, and, although all e-readers will read more than one format, they are not all interchangeable. Table 6.4 shows the major e-readers (at the time of writing) and the e-book formats they work with.

The important thing to take away from Table 6.5 is that if you make e-books available as epub and Mobi files your learners will be able to use them with whatever e-reader they use – unless it's something really exotic and unusual. The other technical thing you need to know is how to do this! Fortunately the industry standard software for pro-ducing e-books is free and fairly intuitive to use. This is Calibre.

Table 6.4 Current major e-readers and their compatible file formats

Hardware	Produced by	Preferred format	Will also read
Kindle	Amazon	.mobi	.pdf .txt .azw
Kobo	Kobo Inc.	.epub	.mobi .pdf .txt
Nook	Barnes & Noble	.epub	.pdf
Sony e-reader	Sony	.lrf	.epub .pdf

Table 6.5 Key app: Calibre

Publisher	Kovid Goval	http://calibre-ebook.com	Licence: Free & open-source
Platform	Windows YES	Mac YES	Linux YES
Also consider	I wouldn't bother – Calibre is well ahead of the game.		
Mobile position	Apps exist for iOS and Android but with reduced functionality, i.e. no conversion between e-book formats		

Figure 6.9 The Calibre interface

To use Calibre to create an e-book you need to start with a document in a suitable file format. Microsoft's proprietary .doc and .docx won't work. You can, however, save a word processing document from Word or Writer in Open Document Format (.odt), Rich Text Format (.rtf) or Portable Document Format (.pdf), and Calibre will convert these to .epub, .mobi, etc., just by adding them to your collection (top left button on Calibre) and converting (third button from the left). Stick the resulting e-book files on your Virtual Learning Environment and – from the technological point of view anyway – you're sorted.

Calibre is an excellent tool for producing and managing e-books; however, it doesn't have an editing facility.

Personalising with technology

If it reads 'burn' as 'bum' you can't change it with Calibre. Fortunately you can use another free tool called Sigil to carry out this kind of editing. Sigil edits e-books in epub format so always use Calibre to make an epub first, then edit in Sigil and convert to any other formats.

Figure 6.10 The Sigil interface

Table 6.6 Key app: Sigil

Publisher	Google	http://code.google.com/p/sigil	Licence: Free & open-source
Platform	Windows YES	Mac YES	Linux YES
Also consider	I wouldn't bother – Sigil is well ahead of the game		
Mobile position	Neither Sigil nor anything like it is available for iOS or Android		

The theory and practice

Learning can take place anywhere. One thing that often limits this is availability of a suitable medium. Being small and highly portable, with very small power requirements, e-book readers and tablets work in a tremendous range of environments.

Figure 6.11 Learning can take place anywhere – especially with an
        e-reader

Some situations where e-book readers are often more
practical than alternatives include:

- on a long school bus journey
- on holiday
- working outdoors in hot weather
- in bed.

E-books also have some technological features that give
them advantages over printed media. Nelson (2008) iden-
tifies dictionaries, pronunciation guides and integrated
multimedia including video, animation and interactive
simulations as features that, in time, are likely to become
standard in e-books. The major barrier to learners adopting
e-books is cultural – people are simply more used to paper

resources. However, a case study from the University of Phoenix shows that learners can be persuaded. The university simply offered students a choice of free e-resources or paid-for handouts. Ninety-nine per cent opted for e-books!

Before leaping in at the deep end and running all our handouts and worksheets through Calibre there are a couple of practical points to bear in mind. It isn't straightforward to convert images and SmartArt into e-book formats. Also there is no point in including interactive elements as you won't be able to fill them in using an e-reader. This means that when you are creating e-books from your existing documents you really have to strip out most of the features that generally make a good text resource. This isn't as contradictory as it sounds – it simply means that the experience of using an e-reader is very different to handling a paper resource and we have to think differently.

Because the use of e-books as a medium for education resources is in its infancy, there is no body of existing good practice to draw upon, so we have to draw on generic pedagogical skills. As with any novel application of technology, try to avoid the 'build it and they will come' trap. However useful e-book formats will be to learners, we need to promote their use and that probably means both class sessions in an IT suite and individual tutorials.

Organising verbal material in visual form

Many of us can benefit from reorganising dense prose into something more visual. There are two approaches to this; mind mapping and concept mapping. Although to the layperson a mind map and a concept map are extremely similar, they have a different theoretical basis and (at least for purists) require different software. Fortunately both are well catered for by free tools.

The technical bit

There are many free tools around for mind mapping and concept mapping. It is also possible – but not necessary – to spend money on these. A good free tool for mind mapping is Freemind; for concept mapping I like VUE (Visual Understanding Environment). VUE has already been reviewed in Chapter 2 (see p. 34). Figure 6.12 shows Freemind. If you prefer an online solution try Mind42 at http://mind42.com.

Figure 6.12 The Freemind interface

Table 6.7 Key app: Freemind

Publisher	Sourceforge	http://freemind. surceforge.net	Licence: Free & open-source
Platform	Windows YES	Mac YES	Linux YES
Also consider	X-Mind, Freeplane		
Mobile position	MinDgo is an Freemind app for both iOS and Android		

Personalising with technology

Freemind allows you to link text, images and a nice set of icons together to create your mind map. Generally mind mapping tools are straightforward to use.

The theory and practice

Concept mapping has already been reviewed on p. 35. Mind maps are a similar idea; like concept maps they are radial diagrams; that is, they begin with a central idea and sub-ideas radiate outwards from this. However, mind maps differ in that all links are radial – unlike in concept maps where extra links between any nodes are encouraged. The other major difference is that concept maps – but not mind maps – tend to specify the nature of a relationship on the link between two nodes.

The idea of using radial diagrams to organise ideas dates back to ancient Greece, but the term 'mind map' has probably been around for a century or so. The current popularity of mind maps owes most to Tony Buzan (1974). Buzan suggests that mind maps work because when we scan a page for information we do so in random sweeps rather than systematically left to right as we have to when reading ordinary text. Buzan suggests that to use a mind map most effectively you should begin with a central idea, move outwards marking connections in several colours and using pictures and/or symbols as well as words where appropriate.

Studies have shown that mind mapping is moderately popular with learners, and that it typically leads to modest improvements in learning. The major proviso here is that there seem to be wide individual differences in how people respond to and benefit from mind mapping. In practice terms this means that, although it is probably worth having all learners experiment with mind maps or concept maps, it probably isn't worth forcing the practice on reluctant learners.

Conclusions and reflections

There is a wealth of technology out there – including much that is free or very low cost – that can transform the format of information so as to play to learners' cognitive strengths and compensate for their weaknesses. In all the recent moves towards personalisation of learning this tends to have been largely forgotten, except where learners' difficulties hit thresholds to trigger funding and expensive tools are provided. Teachers who are highly tech-savvy tend not to be those with a particular interest in personalisation (please don't write in, I know it's a generalisation), and so awareness of the kinds of tools discussed in this chapter is not generally good. Whenever you introduce one of these tools to your learners, be prepared for the fact that the majority probably won't be particularly engaged. However, you may change an individual's whole experience of education. That's got to be worth a shot.

Afterword

Where next for education tech?

Although I hope there will have been a lot of useful stuff for teachers at all levels of ICT competence in this book, in a very real sense the whole idea of a book on technology of any sort is flawed. The sheer pace of technological change means that some things will be obsolete before publication, let alone five years into the life of the book. I wanted to keep this book really practical, though, and so I have focused on what large numbers of teachers in a broad range of contexts can make immediate use of, rather than indulge in a lot of 'blue skies' thinking. The idea of this last mini-chapter is to try to future-proof the book a little and prepare you for some of the likely directions for change over the next few years.

A word about planning for the future

As anyone who has been involved in managing e-learning will know, there is no such thing as a successful one-size-fits-all plan for where to take a school or college in terms of new tech. When people told you five years ago that IWBs were an essential investment they were – with the benefit of hindsight of course – wrong. In the same way, be very cautious now when someone tells you that tablet devices have made interactive whiteboards obsolete or that there is no point in maintaining suites of PCs because all learners prefer to use iPads now. These things are to some extent becoming true for some groups of learners, but they are generalisations, and different teams in different organisations benefit from different solutions. PC suites are still the most convenient solution when a subject has a significant number of learners spending substantial time working on coursework, and teachers of particular subjects and/or learners with particular needs still make really good use of IWBs. Planning needs to take this into account and avoid throwing out babies with bathwater.

That said, technology is changing, and if educational tech is to remain relevant to learners we must keep congruent with the rest of the world. In the current economic climate funding this will require a bit of lateral thinking. With all this in mind, here are my predictions and advice about what developments to keep an eye on.

A changing relationship with the private sector

It is time to move beyond tired stereotypes of private sector ruthlessness and public sector inefficiency. The future will require some mutual respect and imaginative collaboration between the sectors. As regards software, most of the time we can manage perfectly well with free and open-source applications (see Appendix 2 for a discussion of different software licences). We may not need or be able to afford to maintain the kind of software licence fees many schools and colleges currently pay. There are exceptions, of course, and I certainly wouldn't want to be without Dreamweaver or Prezi. It's about understanding when paid-for apps provide something over and above what you can get free.

Although I foresee less money being spent on software licences in the future, there is certainly a role for the private sector in education tech in terms of providing a broader range of hardware and services. At the time of writing some innovative deals are being done whereby private companies provide tablets in bulk for schools and colleges. Staff and in some cases learners can buy these at a discount, staff paying out of their salary. This business model ensures that an organisation can be quickly populated by tablets, allowing the organisation to plan coherently for their pedagogical introduction and securing a high level of teacher 'buy-in'.

Mobile technology and BYOD learning

Technology is becoming increasingly mobile. Globally, desktop and laptop PC sales are falling while numbers of tablets, smartphones and hybrids of the two are rising and set to rise further. Smartphones are clever and powerful devices, and within the lifetime of this book their development will reach a point where they will be able, with a full-size screen and keyboard, to function as a PC. Then BYOD (bring your own device) learning will have truly arrived.

Alternatively, the technology already exists through remote virtualisation (in which an operating system like Windows based on a server is run as a programme on another device such as an Android tablet), a set of tablets can allow a class to do everything they could in a suite of PCs. To implement this just requires the technical expertise to run the virtualisation (the necessary software can be free) and a contract with a company to provide the tablets. Either or both of these solutions will almost certainly reduce the need for large numbers of PCs in schools.

BYOD learning goes hand-in-hand with public-private sector partnership because not all learners will own the right hardware and at least some of this will need to be provided by schools and colleges.

More use of social media

It is hard to picture what the social media of the future will look like but it is safe to say that it will be so integrated into the culture of our learners that it will be impossible for educators to ignore it. We are already at the point where in many contexts a Twitter feed is the most efficient way of communicating with learners. Some commentators are predicting that Web 2.0 has made VLE technology redundant. I would suggest that as VLEs become more interactive and social media more functional the distinction between the two will become a false one.

As we use multiple online social media and other apps, the standard browser set-up may also become dated. Mash-ups (discussed in detail on p. 124) in which we can monitor multiple applications simultaneously and focus down on each as appropriate may become the norm. This mash-up may be via a web service like NetVibes or on the desktop, rather like what was attempted in the design of Windows 8.

Virtual reality and cyborg technology

These are two different directions for technological development but they share a goal of making the human experience of interacting with technology a more complete one by integrating human perception and the technological interface. We experience virtual reality (VR) when we can operate within a three-dimensional world. This can be done on a conventional screen, but the full VR experience requires a 3D interface, for example a virtual reality helmet. The best-known VR environment is Second Life (www.second life.com). This is a complete virtual world where anyone, including educators, can buy land and set up environments such as schools and colleges. There are virtual schools and colleges in Second Life, but it remains to be seen how extensively this kind of environment will be used in the future.

The other route to human-technology integration is cyborg technology. This involves fitting us with devices that boost a human ability or allow us to interface more easily with a machine. There is nothing new about the former idea – pacemakers and hearing aids have been around for a long time. The latter already exists in the form of Bluetooth headsets, but is perhaps a more untapped and interesting possibility in terms of future educational technology. Google glasses are the first mass-production hardware that allow us to view the real world literally through the lens of the virtual world on which we can see data displayed. As with VR it is too early to say what impact this will make on education but the potential, for example, for giving individual real-time feedback is huge. Certainly it is very likely that social media will be viewed in this way.

Concluding comments

That's it! E-learning development plans that try to set out directions for the next three years always look downright silly at the end of the three years because technology moves not only fast but in unpredictable directions. These are my thoughts but they may all – along with those of other pundits – be proved hopelessly wrong! Whatever happens we can be sure that emerging technology will continue to have the potential to improve the learner experience, but also that this is just potential. The art of pedagogy will always override the science of e-learning.

Appendices

1 Sources of further information

Ten information and support websites (with free resources)

This is a selection of free websites featuring software reviews, articles on aspects of e-learning practice, downloadable resources, practice videos and webinars.

	Web address	Description
1	www.jisc.com	Government-sponsored newsletter and free excellent quality advice for colleges and universities*
2	www.ictforeducation.co.uk	Provides free magazine, newsletter and conference programme
3	www.edugeek.net	Very useful articles including reviews of free and low-cost software
4	www.edudemic.com	Useful product reviews and practice articles
5	www.thegeekyteacher.org	Good quality information sheets aimed at non-expert teachers
6	http://elearningeuropa.info	News and articles on all aspects of e-learning

(continued)

Appendices

(continued)

	Web address	Description
7	www.educationworld.com/ a_tech/archives/tools.shtml	Articles and practice tips
8	www.freetech4teachers.com	Nice selection of guides for teachers
9	www.emergingedtech.com	Excellent range of ideas with an emphasis on cutting-edge ideas
10	www.educatorstechnology. com	Large range of good ideas

*Make this your first port of call if you are based at a college or university, and have a browse of the website if you are in a school. JISC provide outstanding support including an analysis of an institution's e-learning needs.

Ten free magazines and journals

This isn't meant to be the most erudite selection of academic journals around, more what is freely available and likely to be of practical help to busy teachers.

	Web address	Title
1	www.ictforeducation.co.uk/docs/ magazine/	ICT for Education
2	http://ijedict.dec.uwi.edu/	International Journalof Education & Development using Information & Communication Technology
3	http://eduscapes.com/activate/ index.html	Activate: the Journal of Technology Rich Learning
4	http://elearnmag.acm.org/index. cfm	eLearn Magazine
5	www.technology-in-education. co.uk/	Technology in Education
6	http://digitallearning.eletsonline. com/	Digital Learning
7	http://acce.edu.au/journal	Australian Educational Computing
8	http://scholar.lib.vt.edu/ ejournals/JTE/v24n2/	Journal of Technology Education

| 9 | http://thejournal.com/ Home.aspx | Large selection of articles and webinars |
| 10 | http://www.elearningage.co.uk/ magazine.aspx | e-Learning Age Magazine |

2 Information about software licensing

This section applies mostly to software that runs on your machine. Some of the online apps can be run on your school or college server, but you as the individual teacher are unlikely to be the one responsible for organising that. The aim of this appendix is to help you understand the different licences that accompany your software. These are important for understanding what you are allowed to run where.

Proprietary and open-source licences

This is the most basic distinction between licence types. Commercial software such as Microsoft Office has a *proprietary* licence. This means that the company that produces the software retain ownership of your copy – what you pay for is to be allowed to use it. In addition your payment only allows you to run it under particular circumstances, for example, on only one machine. If you have paid for commercial software for your own machine, technically you are not supposed to use this copy at work, so plugging your laptop into a school projector is technically a breach of your licence. For some basics like MS Office this shouldn't cause you too many problems as the school or college will almost certainly have a licence too, so you can write documents, presentations, etc., on your machine and run them at work on theirs. However, if you use a lot of proprietary software you may soon find that, while the cost of your individual licences is modest, the cost to the school of keeping up with equivalent site licences is very high.

Open-source licences are very different in the sense that when you download a copy of open-source software you are generally free to do what you like with it, although there may be restrictions on developers altering it and selling it on. In this book I have tried as hard as possible to recommend open-source licences. These have a number of advantages over proprietary licences:

- software is generally free (in the sense that you don't pay anything for it);
- software can generally be run at work as well as on your own machine without any cost to the organisation, and you can give copies to your learners;
- unlike other free software, open-source will almost certainly stay free in the long term;
- if you are or have access to a developer you can alter the software to meet your needs.

The extent to which you need proprietary software depends largely on your subject. If you are involved in teaching ICT, Media or Web Design you will probably find that you will want to use some 'industry standard' applications in order to prepare your learners for the commercial world. A good example is that you will probably want to use Adobe Dreamweaver for web design – this is an outstanding piece of software and I don't mind paying for it. Historically, though, schools and colleges have paid for things where there is a perfectly good free and open-source equivalent.

There is a simple way of evaluating proprietary software: ask yourself two questions. First, does it add value? In other words, is it significantly better in terms of functionality or reliability than a good open-source alternative? Second, is it an industry standard, so you risk disadvantaging your learners' employability if you don't use it? If the answer to either is yes, then look carefully at the cost. If the answer to both is no, don't do it. Also, don't fall into the trap of thinking that proprietary software is always better than open-source. Moodle, Firefox, VLC and Audacity are all open-source programmes that are widely regarded as not just the best *value* in their class but the *best* applications.

'Free' proprietary software

Sometimes you can download software at no cost but it still has a proprietary licence. This comes in various forms:

- *Freeware*: there is no cost, at least for personal use. However, there will still be some restrictions on what you can do with the software. You may also find that what you have is a free cut-down version of something for which you will have to pay if you want a fully featured version. Most freeware is 'real', i.e. it is not a scam, but is not always as good value as it first appears. Beware as well that once freeware reaches a certain level of popularity it often ceases to be free!

- *Shareware*: Shareware licences allow Internet sites to distribute software at no initial cost to the user. What you are getting, however, is some sort of free trial. This is a perfectly reasonable way to try out new software, but be aware that you will be charged at some point, so don't fall into the trap of getting dependent on something without knowing the cost.

3 Fifty(ish) free or very cheap applications you shouldn't be without

As you expand your knowledge of e-learning you will find your own favourites, but this is my 'starter kit' of the sort of applications you will find useful in and around the classroom. Almost everything here is free and most is open-source. Everything is either available for Windows, Mac and Linux users, or there is an equivalent.

Name	Description	Cost
Presentation		
Impress	Open-source PowerPoint clone	Free
Prezi	Non-linear zooming presentation tool	Free online version
VUE	Concept-mapping with presentation mode	Free
Whyteboard	Flipchart simulator	Free
Collabedit	Online collaboration space suitable for presentation feedback and questions	Free
Text processing and simple graphics		
Writer	Open-source Word alternative	Free
Scribus	Desktop publishing	Free
Foxit Reader (Win) Skim (Mac) Xournal (Linux)	PDF annotation	Free
PDFill (Win) JPDFTweak (Mac) PDF Mod (Linux)	PDF split and merge	Free
Picasa	Image manager	Free
Inkscape	Vector graphics editor	Free
Pinta	General graphics editor	Free
Multimedia		
Audacity	Audio recorder and editor	Free
VLC	Media player	Free
Moviemaker (Win) i-Movie (Mac) Openshot (Linux)	Video editor	Free

Camstudio (Win) **Jing (Mac)** **Recordmydesktop (Linux)**	Screencast tool	Free
Animoto	Simple animation	Free
Blender	Complex animation	Free
Pencil	Drawing animation	Free

Online learning

Firefox	Versatile browser with excellent extensions	Free
Chrome	Very fast browser	Free
Google custom search	Programmable Search engine	Free
Moodle	Virtual learning environment	Free
Hot Potatoes	Online quizzes	Free
Dropbox	Online backup and file sharing	Free account available
Mahara	E-portfolio	Free
Twitter	Microblog	Free
Tumblr	Multimedia blog	Free
Wiki Spaces	Wiki builder	Free
Private Social Network	Ning	From £20ish a year
Netvibes	Website mash-up tool	Free account available

Accessibility tools

AT Bar	Web accessibility browser add-on	Free
Browse-aloud (Win) **i-Work text to speech (Mac)** **ReadText (Linux**	Text-to-speech tools	Free Included in iWork package Free
Google Speech Recogniser	Speech to text tool	Free
OpenXML-DAISY	Text to talking book converter	Free
Amis (Windows) **Olearia (Mac)** **DAISY book reader**	DAISY talking book readers	Free Free Free
Calibre	e-book creator	Free
Sigil	e-book editor	Free
Freemind	Mind map generator	Free

References

Auinger, A., Ebner, M., Nedbal, D., Holzinger, A. (2009) Mixing content and endless collaboration MashUps: towards future personal learning environments: universal access in human-computer interaction. *Applications and Services* 14–23.

Bertrancourt, M. (2005) Animation and interactivity principles in multimedia learning, in R. E. Mayer (Ed) *The Cambridge Handbook of Mulitmedia Learning.* Cambridge: Cambrindge University Press.

Buzan, T. (1974) *Use Your Head.* London: BBC Books.

Caruso, J.B. and Kvavik, B. (2005) *Preliminary Results of the 2006 ECAR Study of Students and Information Technology.* Educause Centre for Applied Research.

Churach, D. and Fisher, D. (2001) Science students surf the web: effects on constructivist classroom environments. *Journal of Computers in Mathematics and Science Teaching* 20, 221–247.

Coffield, F., Moseley, D., Hall, E. and Ecclestone, K. (2004) *Should We Be Using Learning Styles? What Research Has to Say to Practice.* London: Learning and Skills Development Agency.

Department for Education (2012) *Teachers' Standards.* London: Department for Education.

Dillenbourg, P. (2000) The promise and performance of course management systems. *ECAR Research Study* 6, 75–85.

Diraa, N., Engelen, J., Ghesquiere, P. and Neyens, K. (2009) *The Use of IT to Support Students with Dyslexia.* USAB 2009, 457–62.

Dodge, B. (1995) *Some Thoughts about Webquests.* Available at: http://webquest.sdsu.edu/about_webquests.html. Accessed 28 September 2010.

Eskicioglu, A.M. and Kopec, D. (2003) *The Ideal Multimedia-Enabled Classroom: A Perspective from Information Science.* Proceedings of the 2003 American Society for Engineering Education Annual Conference & Exposition.

References

Glover, D., Miller, D., Averis, D. and Door, V. (2005) The interactive whiteboard: A literature survey. *Technology, Pedagogy and Education* 14, 155–157.

Higgins, S., Falzon, C.,Hall, I., Moseley, D., Smith, F., Smith, H. and Wall, K. (2005) *Embedding ICT in the Literacy and Numeracy Strategies: Final Report.* Newcastle: Newcastle University.

Jarvis, M. (2011) *Teaching Post-16 Psychology.* London: Routledge.

Jarvis, M., Collins, H. & Gauntlett, L. (2011) Are mash-ups the future for on-line learning platforms? Psychology A-level students' judgements about VLE and MUPPLE interfaces. *Psychology Teaching Review* 17, 83–90.

Kinchington, I.M. (2006) *Increasing the Accessibility of PowerPoint Presentations for those Students Who Do Not Favour Serialist Learning Styles and/or Rote Memorisation,* European Learning Styles Information Network (ELSIN) 11th Annual Conference, 12–14 June, Oslo, Norway.

Maag, M. (2004) The effectiveness of an interactive multimedia learning tool on nursing students' math knowledge and self-efficacy. *CIN: Computers, Informatics, Nursing* 22, 26–33.

Machin, S., McNally, S. and Silva, O. (2007). New technology in schools: Is there a pay-off? *Economic Journal* 117, 1145–1167.

McLoughlin, C. and Lee, M.J.W. (2007) Teaching and learning in the Web 2.0 era: Empowering students through learner-generated content. *Journal of Instructional Technology & Distance Learning* 4, n.p.

Manning, C., Brooks, W., Crotteau, V., Diedrich, A., Moser, J. and Zweifelhofer, A. (2011) Tech tools for teachers, by teachers: Bridging teachers and students. *Wisconsin English Journal* 53, 24–8.

Miller, D., Glover, D. and Averis, D. (2005), 'Presentation and pedagogy: the effective use of interactive whiteboards in mathematics lessons', in D. Hewitt and A. Noyes (Eds), *Proceedings of the sixth British Congress of Mathematics Education held at the University of Warwick*, pp. 105–112.

National Learning Network (2004) Learning Technologies. Available at: www.ccm.ac.uk/ltech/ilt/default.asp. Accessed 9 February 2004.

Nelson, M.R. (2008) E-books in higher education: Nearing the end of the era of hype? *Educause Review* 43, n.p.

Norvig, P. (2003) *The Gettysburg PowerPoint presentation.* Available at: http://norvig.com/Gettysburg. Accessed 28 September 2010.

Novak, J.D. (1964) The importance of conceptual schemes for teaching science. *The Science Teacher* 31, 10–13.

Novak, J.D. and Canas, A.J. (2006) The origins of the concept mapping tool and the continued evolution of the tool. *Information Visualisation Journal* 5, 173–84.

References

Ofsted (2009) *The importance of ICT*. London, Office for Standards in Education.

Ofsted (2011) *ICT in Schools 2008–2011*. London: Office for Standards in Education.

Ofsted (2012) *The Framework for School Inspection*. London: Office for Standards in Education.

O'Reilly, T. (2005) Web 2.0: compact definition. O'Reilly Radar (blog). O'Reilly Media.

Paivio, A. (1971) *Imagery and Cognitive Processes*. New York: Holt, Rinehart & Winston.

Papert, S. (1996) *The Connected Family: Bridging the Digital Generation Gap*. Atlanta, GA: Longstreet Press.

Selinger, M. (2001) The role of the teacher: Teacherless classrooms? In M. Leask (ed.) *Issues in Teaching Using ICT*. London: Routledge.

Selwyn, N. (2007) Web 2.0 applications as alternative environments for informal learning: A critical review. Paper delivered at OECD-KERIS expert meeting.

Suri, H. & Schuhmacher, M. (2008) *Open-source vs proprietary VLE: an exploratory study of staff perceptions*. Melbourne: Proceedings ascilite.

Taraaghi, B., Ebner, M. and S. Schaffert (2009) Personal Learning Environments for Higher education: a Mashup-based widget concept, Proceedings of the 2nd Int. Workshop on Mashup Personal Learning Environments (MUPPLE09), Nice, France.

Tufte, E. (2004) PowerPoint is evil. *Wired* 9, n.p.

Turker, M.A. and Zingel, S. (2008) Formative interfaces for scaffolding self-regulated learning in PLEs. *E-Learning Papers* 9, 1–15.

Index

Index

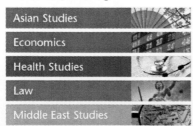
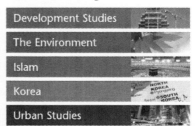